containment

containment

Rebuilding a Strategy
against Global Terror

Ian Shapiro

PRINCETON UNIVERSITY PRESS

PRINCETON AND OXFORD

Requests for permission to reproduce material from this work should be sent to Permissions, Princeton University Press

Published by Princeton University Press, 41 William Street, Princeton, New Jersey 08540

In the United Kingdom: Princeton University Press, 3 Market Place, Woodstock, Oxfordshire OX20 1SY

LIBRARY OF CONGRESS CATALOGING-IN-PUBLICATION DATA

Shapiro, Ian.
   Containment : rebuilding a strategy against global terror / Ian Shapiro.
     p. cm.
   Includes bibliographical references and index.
   ISBN-13: 978-0-691-12928-0 (hardcover : alk. paper)
   ISBN-10: 0-691-12928-2 (hardcover : alk. paper)
   1. Terrorism—Prevention—Government policy—United States.
2. National security—United States—History—20th century.   I. Title.
   HV6432.S49   2007
   363.325'170973—dc22   2006031331

British Library Cataloging-in-Publication Data is available

This book has been composed in Bembo and Franklin Gothic

Printed on acid-free paper. ∞

press.princeton.edu

Printed in the United States of America

10 9 8 7 6 5 4 3 2 1

For Xan Shapiro

ASPIRING INTERNATIONAL DIPLOMAT

Contents

Preface

I backed into writing this book in a curious way. In September of 2004 I was asked to give a lecture to the Yale Club of Tokyo. I supplied a list of possible topics, but my host, Jim Brooke, rejected them all, saying that his members wanted me to talk instead about what a Kerry administration's foreign policy would be. This prompted me to give a lecture on why there was not going to be a Kerry administration, out of which the book grew. My expectations about the Kerry campaign flowed from the conviction that in politics it is hard to beat something with nothing.

The Democrats had been on the defensive since the Republican sweep of Congress for the first time in a generation ten years earlier. That takeover had mainly been driven by domestic politics. Democrats were unready for the assault on the welfare state and the tax-cutting juggernaut that had been incubating in the Heritage Foundation, the American Enterprise Institute, and other conservative think tanks since the 1970s. Codified in the House Republicans' 1994 manifesto, the *Contract with America*, the new Republican agenda recast political debate in Washington with Democrats scrambling to get aboard. By 1996 President Clinton had become a budget-balancing fiscal conservative and was signing legislation to "end welfare as we know it." When George W. Bush came into office in January of 2001, conservatives moved quickly to consolidate their gains, passing colossal tax cuts aimed at the wealthiest Americans. These were enacted with broad bipartisan support in Congress, reflecting the extent to which the Democrats had been co-opted by the new conservative program.[1]

Foreign policy had not figured prominently in the 2000 presidential election campaign. The 1990s had been America's decade internationally. The glow of the post–Cold War jubilation burned strong. The European Union was incorporating much of the old Soviet bloc. Russia was being welcomed as an American ally. China was embracing capitalism with the zeal of a convert and opening itself to American investment. The decades-long conflict in Northern Ireland seemed on its way to resolution. Apartheid had disappeared peacefully from South Africa. Serious problems of pollution, poverty, and disease—especially AIDS— remained to be tackled, but geopolitically the world seemed benign. Attempts to resolve the conflict in the Middle East might have failed. But this was scarcely new, and the conflict showed no signs of expanding or of spinning out of control.

True, terrorist activity had been directed against the United States throughout the decade. An attempt to blow up the World Trade Center in New York City by placing explosives in its underground parking garages failed in 1993. Six civilians died. The U.S. embassies in Nairobi and Dar es Salaam were bombed in 1998, leaving 259 people dead. The USS *Cole* was attacked in Yemen two years later, killing seventeen members of the ship's crew. Osama bin Laden and Al Qaeda were implicated in these attacks. But the Clinton administration was distracted by the Monica Lewinsky scandal, and few people, if any, joined the dots to conclude that the United States faced fundamentally new threats that should lead to a basic reorientation in its dealings with the rest of the world.

Vice President Al Gore structured his unsuccessful 2000 campaign around running away from the Clinton administration's scandals, taking credit for its successes, and proving that he was "my own man."[2] His international pronouncements had mainly to do with the environment. George W. Bush focused his campaign on domestic policy, principally tax cuts. He made the standard Republican noises about avoiding unnecessary foreign entanglements and insisting on overwhelming force and clear exit strategies should they become unavoidable. He poured scorn on the idea of nation building. Once he became president, his early national security actions had to do with reviving Ronald Reagan's Star Wars missile defense system and slimming down the conventional military—for which purpose Donald Rumsfeld was named secretary of defense.

9/11 changed all that. If the Democrats had been blindsided by the speed with which House Speaker Newt Gingrich redefined the domestic political agenda after 1994, they were positively stampeded by the foreign policy transformation after the September 2001 attacks. In tandem with the sea changes that had been planned in conservative think tanks for domestic policy, a great deal of groundwork had been done on foreign policy. The neoconservatives, as they became known, rejected the isolationist tradition of the mainstream Republican Party out of hand, supporting instead the aggressive export of American democratic capitalism and values around the world. Commentators like Irving Kristol, David Frum, and Richard Perle worked hard to market their ideas to the chattering classes and on Capitol Hill. But few Democrats took them seriously before 9/11.

The Clinton administration had resisted the neoconservative arguments and pressure, and the first months of the new Bush administration had been dominated by the tax-cutting agenda. But the neoconservatives enjoyed close links to Rumsfeld, his deputy, Paul Wolfowitz, and to Vice President Dick Cheney. These links paid huge dividends after the 9/11 attacks. While the American military pursued Osama bin Laden and the Taliban in Afghanistan, in Washington pressure quickly built to seize the moment to topple Saddam Hussein's regime in Iraq and begin transforming the Middle East. The neoconservative credo became U.S. policy virtually overnight, defended in a series of speeches by President Bush and other senior administration officials in 2002. It was codified in the *National Security Strategy of the United States of America*, published by the White House in September of that year and reaffirmed in a similar document three and a half years later.[3]

The purposes of the Iraq war were murky from the start. It was sold as essential to deal with weapons of mass destruction with which Saddam Hussein allegedly threatened his people, his neighbors, the United States, and the world. Subsidiary war aims, to end internal repression in Iraq and achieve "regime change," took on increasing momentum as the weapons of mass destruction failed to materialize following the invasion in March of 2003. Few hard questions had been asked of the administration in the run-up to the conflict, despite the fact that there was no plausible evidence linking Iraq to the 9/11 attacks or to Al Qaeda. The Democrats were on the run, lacking ideas of their own and afraid to challenge a popular president during wartime. Congress supported the administration's policy with strong bipartisan votes in the fall of 2002. Resolutions authorizing the president to go to war in Iraq passed the House by 296 to 133 votes and the Senate by 77 to 23.

It was not until the war started going badly that Democratic criticism began in earnest. It failed to gain much traction through the 2004 presidential campaign, not least because so many Democrats were deeply implicated in the decision to go to war. Massachusetts Democratic candidate Senator John Kerry became politically hamstrung during the campaign by his convoluted assertion about Iraq war funding that "I actually did vote for the $87 billion before I voted against it," and by his insistence that his 2002 vote to authorize President Bush to go to war did not amount to a vote for the war. He spent much of the rest of his campaign trying to explain what he had meant by these assertions.[4] This was emblematic of the degree to which critics of the administration's national security strategy could not tell a coherent story about what they favored.

After the 2004 U.S. election Iraq descended into civil war.[5] As a result, criticism of the administration has intensified. Yet conspicuously missing from the American public debate has been serious discussion of alternatives to the Bush administration's dealings with the rest of the world in the name of national security. There has been plenty of criticism, much of it valid, of the Iraq invasion and its aftermath, and of the administration's policies toward Iran, North Korea, and other strategic adversaries. But almost all of it has been ad hoc, focused on the competence of the players. The United States stands in manifest need of a national security doctrine that can be appealing to the American electorate, defensible in the court of international public opinion, and attractive to America's democratic allies. In this book I make the case that, suitably modified for the post-9/11 world, the doctrine of containment developed at the outset of the Cold War meets this need better than the Bush Doctrine or any other going alternative.

On learning that I was writing a book on the containment of threats to America's survival as a democracy, one colleague remarked that perhaps I should start with the current occupants of 1600 Pennsylvania Avenue. The erosion of democratic liberties that has been perpetrated in the name of national security since 9/11 is indeed serious. Nor is it restricted to the United States. In the aftermath of July 7, 2005, bombings in London, the *Economist* attacked both the Blair government and Tory opposition for adopting draconian new limits on "inflammatory" speech—even though Britain already had among the toughest antiterror legislation in the democratic world. "Free speech is not a privilege," it was noted, "to be revoked if it is misused, but a pillar of democracy."[6]

We should all be worried when editorial writers at the *Economist* complain that democracy is being eroded from within. Many journalists, scholars, and public intellectuals on both sides of the Atlantic are speaking out on these issues. I applaud their efforts, but they are not my principal focus here. My goal is to spell out an alternative to the Bush national security doctrine and show why that alternative should be embraced. It is rooted in our best national security and democratic traditions. It offers the best available hope for protecting the American people and their democracy into the future, and for restoring our government's moral and political legitimacy at home and abroad. It complements the defense of civil liberties, and concerns about internal erosion of democracy, on which others have focused.

Nor is this a book about how to extricate the United States from Iraq. I have a good deal to say in these pages about our involvement there, some of which has implications for our current dilemmas on the ground. In both Afghanistan and Iraq the administration has failed to grasp how much democratic nation building depends for its legitimacy on domestic grassroots support. This does not mean that sustainable democratic institutions can never be created by an outside power. We know from the examples of postwar Japan and West Germany that sometimes they can be. But doing this requires careful efforts to build local legitimacy for the fledgling institutions, efforts that have not been made in Afghanistan or Iraq. Indeed, many of the difficulties in Iraq can be traced to the fact that the U.S.-led coalition forces have ignored or overruled elected local leaders, insisting on imposing solutions on them instead.[7]

I also explain why developing a viable post-occupation containment strategy in Iraq requires that we set a definite date for the departure of American troops. However, this is not primarily a book about what to do in Iraq now. Its goal, rather, is to ensure that we do not become entangled in the next Iraq—be this in Iran, Syria, North Korea, or elsewhere. Unless U.S. national security policy is rescued from the clutches of those who fashioned the Bush Doctrine, and rethought from the ground up, the danger is that the wrong lessons will be drawn from the Iraq conflict and its fallout. Our democracy and moral standing in the world will be eroded further, and our national security will be placed in even greater jeopardy than it is now. *Containment: Rebuilding a Strategy against Global Terror* is intended to foster and contribute to that rethinking, helping set America on a better course.

1   The Idea Vacuum

Power expands to fill a vacuum. This holds for ideas no less than for military campaigns, as the George W. Bush administration's national security doctrine has so dramatically underscored.[1] Announced in the wake of the September 11, 2001, attacks on the World Trade Center and the Pentagon, it ranks as one of the most dramatic sea changes in U.S. national security policy ever. The Bush Doctrine has also turned traditional Republican Party foreign policy inside out and upside down. The congenital skeptics of foreign entanglements, whose leader heaped scorn on "nation building" in his 2000 presidential campaign, were transformed overnight into the world's self-appointed internationalists and policemen. The Bush administration committed itself to exporting American-style freedom and democracy worldwide, to confronting an "Axis of Evil" that was said to reach from to Tehran to Pyongyang, and to waging unilateral preemptive war by coalitions "of the willing" so as to achieve regime change as was undertaken in Iraq in March of 2003.

A good part of the Bush Doctrine's easy ascendancy can be explained by the shock, scale, and sheer drama of the 9/11 attacks that unfolded in excruciating detail on live television on that beautiful September morning, killing more civilians than had the Japanese bombing of Pearl Harbor sixty years earlier. It created an opening for Vice

President Cheney, Defense Secretary Donald Rumsfeld, and his influential neoconservative deputy Paul Wolfowitz to rewrite American national security policy almost overnight, without any serious debate on Capitol Hill or any significant opposition from the Democrats.

The Florida election debacle in November of 2000 brought George W. Bush to office with less legitimacy than any president since John Quincy Adams.[2] By the time of the 2002 midterm elections, however, his standing was sufficiently enhanced that the Republicans gained seats in both houses of Congress, bucking the usual pattern whereby the party controlling the White House loses seats on Capitol Hill. The Republican congressional majorities grew again in 2004.[3] Moreover, President Bush erased the dead heat of his contest with Al Gore by winning a majority of close to three million in the popular vote over Democratic challenger John Kerry. The administration's reduced popularity took its toll on Capitol Hill in the 2006 midterm elections, but the Bush White House remained in firm control of the national security agenda.

By the time of the 2004 presidential election the original rationale for the Iraq war was in tatters. It was obvious to all that the widely touted weapons of mass destruction did not exist. Nor was there any evidence of a reconstituted nuclear program. President Bush had been forced to admit that there was no link between Iraq and the 9/11 attacks. The war itself was going badly, with more than a thousand American combat troops dead, some multiple of that number wounded, and no plausible exit strategy—not to mention actual exit—in sight. Yet a decorated war veteran could not unseat an administration that had abandoned its core national security principles and bungled a reckless war of choice. Kerry played into the administration's hands by turning the spotlight from the start onto the wrong war—the last war—by declaring that he was "reporting for duty" and flaunting his Vietnam past and buddies at the Democratic National Convention in Boston. The result was months of charges and countercharges about whether Kerry had won his medals honorably, whether he had faked throwing them over the White House fence, whether he had called his comrades war criminals in his antiwar congressional testimony in the early 1970s, and whether he had misrepresented other aspects of his war record.

When Kerry did confront Bush over the conduct of the Iraq war, there was no contest of ideas or principles. The charges were over gullibility in believing the claims of Ahmed Chalabi and others that Americans would be greeted with flowers in the streets as liberators, over poor postwar planning, over lack of adequate equipment for the troops and armor for trucks, and over other matters of fundamental competence. Kerry did describe the conflict as "the wrong war in the wrong place at the wrong time," but he was handicapped by having voted to authorize it in the Senate—a vote based, as the Bush campaign never tired of pointing out, on his having seen the same national intelligence estimates (NIE) that they had seen.[4] This reduced Kerry to parsing the differences between voting to authorize war and deciding to go to war. Such distinctions are too subtle for electoral politics, where everyone knows that once you are explaining you are losing—if you have not already lost. It was as if Kerry had never noticed how disastrously Michael Dukakis had failed against George Bush's father in 1988, when Dukakis declared that "this election isn't about ideology. It's about competence."[5]

Or perhaps, as I contend here, the problem was that Kerry focused on tactical attacks on the Bush administration's competence because he lacked his own strategic vision of U.S. national security. The first rule of electoral politics is that you can't beat something with nothing. Particularly when one is confronting an administration that is as explicitly and dramatically ideologically driven as the George W. Bush administration, it is essential to formulate an alternative and demonstrate its superiority and attractiveness.

My goal here is to do just that. I begin with an account of the ideological vacuum created by the 9/11 attacks, which obliterated the possibility of thinking about counterterrorism through the lens of the criminal justice system. In chapter 3, I chronicle how the Bush administration filled this vacuum with the Bush Doctrine and its "war on terror," illustrating how radical a departure this has been not only from traditional Republican and conservative ideas in recent American politics, but also from U.S. national security practices at least since the days of Woodrow Wilson. In chapters 4–6, my attention shifts to defending a credible alternative to the Bush Doctrine.

My argument depends centrally on adapting the doctrine of containment developed by George Kennan, a career foreign service diplomat and then director of the Policy Planning Staff for President Truman, in response to the emerging Soviet threat after World War II. Kennan's argument was laid out in "The Sources of Soviet Conduct," published in *Foreign Affairs* in 1947, signed by "X," but widely known to have been his work.[6] It provided the basis for the Truman administration's early postwar approach to the Soviet Union. Although it was modified in a variety of ways by Truman and his successors, the core ideas structured U.S. national security policy for much of the Cold War. The architects of the Bush Doctrine have declared containment to be obsolete in the post-9/11 era. I show that they are wrong. Refashioning containment in light of the realities of the twenty-first century offers the best bet for securing Americans from violent attack while preserving democracy at home and diffusing it abroad.

Kennan believed two things about the Soviets: that appeasement of their ambitions would be disastrous for America's vital interests, and that a direct assault on the USSR or its client states was unnecessary and would be counterproductive. The dangers of appeasement required no extended defense in the aftermath of World War II. Containment was intended to prevent Soviet expansion without saddling the United States with unsustainable global military obligations. It committed the United States to war only when its vital interests are at stake. Otherwise, the Soviet threat was to be contained by our relying on economic sticks and carrots, fostering competition within the world communist movement, engaging in diplomacy, promoting the health and vitality of the capitalist democracies, and ensuring that our attempts to combat the Soviets would not make us become more like them. As the Soviets became overextended internationally and the dysfunctional features of their economic system played themselves out, patient application of these tools would be sufficient to guarantee America's national security.

The Soviet adversary that concerned Kennan posed different challenges from those faced by the United States in the post-9/11 world, but there are important similarities as well. Kennan's article, initially known as the "Long

Telegram," began as a February 1946 State Department cable from Moscow. It was designed to convince his superiors that the USSR's political outlook was so antithetical to ours that the United States had to find a basis for dealing with the Soviets other than argument and persuasion. Sometimes they might go through the motions of talking, but Kennan insisted that they saw the arguments of Western governments as mere ideological rationalizations for a system they utterly rejected as exploitative, decadent, and subversive of the world they sought to create.

The parallels with the architects of 9/11 and their supporters do not end there. Kennan had no doubt that the Soviets had regional, if not global, ambitions, that they were constitutionally hostile to democracy as Americans understood it, and that they expected much of the ideological contest between their system and ours to be played out in the Third World. And just as defenders of containment had to face down critics who sought to equate it with appeasement during the Cold War, so I argue here that today containment offers better and more powerful tools than does the Bush Doctrine for protecting Americans and their democracy.

Moreover, though this was not Kennan's focus, Islamic fundamentalists share in common with the old Soviets the lack of a viable economic model or a success story to which they can point. Where they have come to power, in countries like Afghanistan and Iran, the economic results have been disastrous because authoritarian regimes are not good at running market economies. In Saudi Arabia, a more complex example, success depends entirely on a nonrenewable resource. This makes it doubtful that in the medium term they can pose a serious challenge to democratic capitalism. For these reasons, among others, I make the case here that Kennan's arguments for containment have continuing relevance to our present circumstances.

There are, nonetheless, significant differences between the world the United States and its allies faced during the Cold War and the adversaries we confront today. The most obvious concerns the object of containment. The Soviet Union was a single "it," whereas today we face dangerous threats from a variety of hostile regimes and transnational terrorist groups. In one respect, as I argue, this situation lends itself to containment. It creates tensions among our adversaries' agendas, as well as openings for competition among them. But containing threats to America's survival as a democracy also confronts us with less predictable, more fluid and open-ended challenges than we faced in the Cold War. This reality is compounded by the proliferation of nuclear and other weapons of mass destruction. The world is less stable than it was for much of the Cold War.

Recognizing this does not give us good reasons to abandon containment, but it does make it more complicated. It also suggests the importance of international instruments for which Kennan had little time. Among these are international law and institutions. The challenges posed by weak states, transnational terrorist groups, and unpredictable alliances all suggest that we should buttress the institutions of international legitimacy—pressing them into the service of fostering democracy, and containing threats to it, as best we can. And, whereas Kennan opposed collective defense arrangements like NATO, we should recognize that they can sometimes be helpful tools of containment—so long as they remain subordinate to our vital interest in securing the American people and their democracy into the future.[7] It is ironic, as we will see, that the two areas where the Bush administration's practice has come closest to Kennan's views are the two areas where they stand in most need of modification.

One other parallel with the early Cold War years deserves mention. Since the collapse of the Soviet empire, Kennan and containment have deservedly been accorded great credit for the national security stance that contributed so much to that result without a superpower war. It is worth noting, however, that at the start of the Cold War it was no foregone conclusion that containment would be the dominant strategy. In the 1952 election campaign Dwight Eisenhower attacked containment. His future secretary of state, John Foster Dulles, called for "rollback" of the Soviet Union in Eastern Europe, and for aggressive confrontation with communism worldwide. That these views did not prevail, even in the Eisenhower administration, is due, in part at least, to the fact that they were vigorously contested by containment's defenders.

This history makes the Democrats' failure to contest the Bush Doctrine in the present climate, and to get behind an alternative like that proposed here, all the more troubling. This subject is taken up in chapter 7. The Democrats' failure can be traced to several sources. One is fear of challenging a president in a time of national crisis. A second, on the left of the Democratic Party, stems from ideological discomfort with the very idea of national security policy. A third is rooted in the changes wrought in the party's ideology by the Democratic Leadership Council (DLC) since the 1980s and the resulting tactical political imperatives. Yet unless the DLC outlook is fundamentally rethought, the Democrats are unlikely to find an effective vehicle to challenge the Bush Doctrine in the medium term. Even if they win the White House in 2008, they will likely have been co-opted by much of the Bush administration's self-defeating national security policy.

In July of 2005, in the course of sentencing Algerian "millennium bomber" Ahmed Ressam to twenty-two years in prison for planning to detonate a bomb at Los Angeles International Airport, U.S. District Judge John C. Coughenour went out of his way to explain that the federal courts are equal to the task of prosecuting suspected terrorists. "I would like to convey the message that our system works," he said. "We did not need to use a secret military tribunal, or detain the defendant indefinitely as an enemy combatant, or deny him the right to counsel, or invoke any proceedings beyond those guaranteed by or contrary to the United States Constitution." Judge Coughenour insisted that the message "to the world" from the proceedings was that "our courts have not abandoned our commitment to the ideals that set our nation apart. We can deal with the threats to our national security without denying the accused fundamental constitutional protections." In a scarcely disguised slap at the Bush administration's response to terrorism, he added: "Unfortunately, some believe that this threat renders our Constitution obsolete. This is a Constitution for which men and women have died and continue to die and which has made us a model among nations. If that view is allowed to prevail, the terrorists will have won."[1]

Judge Coughenour's remarks reflect his dismay at the collapse of the widespread pre-9/11 consensus that terrorism should be dealt with through the criminal justice system. To be sure, military and foreign intelligence services have always been involved in counterterrorism, but until 9/11 this involvement basically resembled their contribution to international drug interdiction. Presidents from Nixon to Reagan periodically declared wars "on drugs," but no one took these to be wars in a literal sense that would require congressional declarations or trigger executive power to mobilize troops. Nor did anyone think they would involve dealing with drug traffickers as anything other than criminals. Traffickers were tried in criminal courts bound by conventional criminal procedures, and, when convicted, they received criminal penalties in the usual way. When they were apprehended outside the United States, attempts were made to extradite them or, failing that, to ensure that they would be prosecuted as criminals in other countries. Terrorism is not even a candidate for prosecution in international tribunals or the International Criminal Court, which are reserved for gross human rights abuses committed by government officials.

The criminal justice approach to terrorism did not brook partisan disagreement before 9/11. Republicans never dissented from the prosecution and sentencing of the terrorists who attacked the World Trade Center in 1993. Even when Osama bin Laden began to emerge as a threat of a different order—setting his sights on overtly political targets such as the U.S. embassies in Kenya and Tanzania that were bombed in 1998, and even military targets such as the USS *Cole*, attacked in Yemen in two years later—there was no call to militarize the general antiterrorism effort. To be sure, the military would engage in the occasional retaliatory strike, as Ronald Reagan had done after 241 marines were killed by a car bomb outside their Beirut barracks in October of 1983, or when he ordered the bombing of Tripoli in retaliation for Libya's alleged complicity in the terrorist bombing of the La Belle discothèque in West Berlin in April of 1986. But no one suggested that such strikes were or should be part of a fundamentally new approach to terrorism. Indeed, after 9/11 it came to light that, until the planes struck, career professionals in the Justice and Defense departments had been frustrated by their inability to get relevant executive officials in the new administration to focus on terrorist threats. Those officials were notably more interested in a new round of Star Wars funding and downsizing the conventional military than in counterterrorism.[2]

The pre-9/11 consensus on the criminal justice approach to terrorism is scarcely surprising. Even when they have harbored more or less well-defined territorial ambitions, terrorist groups are by definition not governments. In the living memory of most people in the West in the 1990s, "terrorism" conjured up groups like Bader-Meinhof, the PLO, the IRA, and Basque separatists. People might experience ambivalence about groups that employed terror tactics against brutal governments of questionable legitimacy, summed up in the adage that one person's terrorist is another's freedom fighter. But even in that case, few, other than their members perhaps, saw such groups as legitimate governments in exile. Significant levels of domestic political support for such groups, as with the IRA in the United States, might have resulted in lackluster enforcement of interdiction for fund-raising and related activities by U.S. authorities. But this was a far cry from removing terrorism from the purview of the criminal law.

That governments treated terrorism as a criminal matter is understandable and, indeed, desirable also because it denies its proponents what they most seek: political legitimacy. Criminals lack even the pretense of a political justification for their actions. This was underscored by the amnesty legislation enforced by the South African Truth and Reconciliation Commission, which required applicants for amnesty to convince the commission that they had acted from a political motive.[3] Portraying violent groups as criminal thus had its advantages so long as the damage they inflicted, and the casualties they wrought, were comparatively minor. Indeed, even when 168 people were killed by a bomb planted outside the Oklahoma City Federal Building by antigovernment activists in April 1995, the political motive (alleged retaliation for the attack by federal agents on the Branch Davidian cult in Waco, Texas, two years earlier) did not prevent the perpetrators, Timothy McVeigh and Terry Nichols, from being tried and convicted as criminals.

The possibility of treating terrorism as crime evaporated on 9/11 not only because of the sheer scale of the attacks, but also because they were a simultaneous onslaught on the most visible facets of America's commercial, military, and political infrastructure.[4] It would be hard to imagine a more blatant assault on a nation's public identity; certainly the 9/11 attacks dwarfed anything that had hitherto been conjured up in Hollywood. Moreover, it quickly transpired that the Al Qaeda terrorist group led by Osama bin Laden that was responsible for the attacks was harbored by the Taliban government in Afghanistan. The Taliban leader, Mullah Omar, openly defied the September 18, 2001, UN Security Council resolution requiring him to close all terrorist training camps immediately and reaffirming an earlier demand that the Taliban hand over Osama bin Laden to the United States or a third party for trial for the African embassy bombings.[5] Omar's defiance reinforced the sense that the attacks were a warlike act, even if they were not themselves actually perpetrated by an army controlled by a government. As a result, the United States enjoyed widespread international support when it invaded Afghanistan with help primarily from the United Kingdom, Australia, Canada, and the indigenous Afghan opposition Northern Alliance. Indeed the UN General Assembly agreed with the Security Council and Secretary-General Kofi Annan that the invasion was legitimate under Chapter VII, Article 51, of the UN Charter.[6] The "war on terror" had started.

3   Filling the Vacuum

For all the talk about the clash of civilizations in the academy and about Islamofascism on right-wing radio talk shows, during the first four years the Bush Doctrine was not portrayed by the administration as a response to Islam, or even a response to militant Islam.[1] In the immediate aftermath of the 9/11 attacks, President Bush was careful to declare that "the enemy of America is not our many Muslim friends. It is not our many Arab friends. Our enemy is a radical network of terrorists and every government that supports them."[2] Indeed, the Bush Doctrine was not billed as a response to any particular ideology. The "Axis of Evil" identified in the State of the Union address four months after the 9/11 attacks included the Islamic theocracy in Iran, communist North Korea, and Saddam Hussein's secular Ba'thist regime then in control of Iraq.[3] Rather, the doctrine, codified in the new *National Security Strategy of the United States of America* published eight months later, was described as a response to a particular type of military threat— a combination of tactics and weaponry revolving around the use of terror. The central principles of the Bush Doctrine were reiterated in a second *National Security Strategy*, published three and a half years later.

President Bush set the tone for the *National Security Strategy* at his West Point commencement speech in June of 2002 by insisting that the twin pillars of the U.S. strategy in the Cold War—the doctrines of deterrence and containment—are not equal to threats confronting America today. "Deterrence—the promise of massive retaliation against nations—means nothing against shadowy terrorist networks with no nation or citizens to defend," Bush insisted. And containment is impossible when "unbalanced dictators with weapons of mass destruction can deliver those weapons on missiles or secretly provide them to terrorist allies."[4] Vice President Cheney followed up in August, reiterating that the United States has entered "a struggle of years" in which "old doctrines of security do not apply." During the Cold War, Cheney continued, the United States could manage the threat with strategies of deterrence and containment. "But it's a lot tougher to deter enemies who have no country to defend, and containment is not possible when dictators obtain weapons of mass destruction and are prepared to share them with terrorists, who intend to inflict catastrophic casualties on the United States."[5]

The 2002 *National Security Strategy* is built upon, and extends, these remarks. It starts from the premise that "new deadly challenges have emerged from rogue states and terrorists." They might not rival the Soviet Union's "sheer destructive power," but the Soviets thought of weapons of mass destruction (WMD) as weapons of last resort, whereas these new enemies do not. They have created a more "complex and dangerous" national security environment owing to their "determination to obtain destructive powers hitherto available only to the world's strongest states, and the greater likelihood that they will use weapons of mass destruction against us."[6] It has taken "almost a decade for us to comprehend the true nature of this new threat." Now that it is clear, "the United States can no longer solely rely on a reactive posture as we have in the past. The inability to deter a potential attacker, the immediacy of today's threats, and the magnitude of potential harm that could be caused by our adversaries' choice of weapons, do not permit that option. We cannot let our enemies strike first."[7]

Six defining features of the Bush Doctrine underscore how radical a departure it is from Republican orthodoxy and prior American national security policy. The first concerns its worldwide scope. The 2002 *National Security Strategy* asserts the right of the United States to act militarily anywhere in the world on the grounds that the United States "is fighting a war against terrorists of global reach."[8] In January 2003, in the run-up to the Iraq invasion, Vice President Cheney insisted that confronting Iraq "is not a distraction from the war on terror, it is absolutely crucial to winning the war on terror." This was because it "would take just one vial, one canister, one crate to bring a day of horror to our nation unlike any we have ever known."[9] In the fall of 2003, following the invasion, Defense Secretary Donald Rumsfeld reiterated that the way "to defeat terrorists is to take the war to them—to go after them where they live and plan and hide, and make clear to states that sponsor and harbor them that such actions will have consequences."[10] The 2006 *National Security Strategy* echoes this commitment.[11]

Before the advent of the Bush Doctrine, no U.S. government had ever asserted a right to act militarily anywhere in the world. The closest any administration had come was the Monroe Doctrine. Coined by President James Monroe's secretary of state, John Quincy Adams, in 1823, it asserted America's right to resist any expansion of European imperialism in the New World "as dangerous to our peace and safety."[12] In principle this included the entire Western Hemisphere, but in practice the Monroe Doctrine was taken seriously only in close proximity to the mainland of North and South America.[13] The Bush Doctrine, by contrast, is the Monroe Doctrine on crack. The 2002 *National Security Strategy* asserts America's right to act militarily anywhere in the world. The United States will defend itself against terrorists and rogue states identified as threats to "the United States, the American people, and our interests at home and abroad by identifying and destroying the threat before it reaches our borders."[14] The Iraq war made it plain that the doctrine is intended to be acted on. Baghdad is eight time zones from the east coast of the United States. Lest there be any doubt that nowhere is off-limits in the battle against the "Axis of Evil," Pyongyang is twelve time zones away. The only way to get farther away from the east coast of the United States is by blasting off into space.

To be sure, the United States made military commitments across the globe long before 9/11. American troops went to Korea in 1950, and the United States became more widely embroiled in Southeast Asia in the following decade. Turkey, also in Baghdad's time zone, has been a member of NATO since 1952. It could trigger U.S. involvement there if attacked. The Clinton administration bombed Kosovo in 1999. By the end of the twentieth century the United States had troops stationed in perhaps a hundred countries around the globe.

Yet all this fell short of any assertion of a U.S. right to act militarily anywhere in the world. The action in Korea was at the behest of the UN Security Council (then being boycotted by the Soviet Union). American involvement in

Vietnam—scarcely a model for the future, as I argue later—was at the behest of the South Vietnamese. The commitment to Turkey is a treaty obligation. The action in Kosovo was indeed of questionable legitimacy as we will see, but it was defended as a humanitarian intervention and was in any case a NATO operation that avoided the use of American ground troops.[15] American forces have, of course, engaged in clandestine activities around the world to further the agendas of various U.S. administrations. But the very fact that these activities had to be clandestine underscores their impropriety.

The Bush Doctrine is unequivocal, second, in affirming a right to unilateral action that is unconstrained by traditional alliances. "While the United States will constantly strive to enlist the support of the international community," the 2002 *National Security Strategy* asserts, "we will not hesitate to act alone, if necessary."[16] The document genuflects toward taking international obligations "seriously" and making use of allies and international institutions, but is insistent that "coalitions of the willing can augment these permanent institutions."[17] Coalitions of the willing can be drawn from anywhere to fight particular battles. As early as November 2001, President Bush made it clear that "[a] coalition partner must do more than just express sympathy, a coalition partner must perform. That means different things for different nations. Some nations don't want to contribute troops and we understand that. Other nations can contribute intelligence-sharing. . . . But all nations, if they want to fight terror, must do something."[18]

A third radical innovation concerns recasting the policy of preemptive war. President Truman had described preemptive wars as "weapons of dictators, not of free democratic countries like the United States."[19] His view was echoed in the National Security Council's memorandum of 1950 that set the basic terms of U.S. national security policy during the Cold War. "It goes without saying that the idea of 'preventive' war—in the sense of a military attack not provoked by a military attack upon us or our allies—is generally unacceptable to Americans." NSC-68 goes on to note that although some people advocate preventive war nonetheless, their arguments should be rejected as impractical and "morally corrosive." Victory in such a war would come at so great a cost in lost moral legitimacy at home and abroad that it would bring the United States "little if at all closer to victory in the fundamental ideological conflict" with the Soviet Union.[20]

By contrast, President Bush's 2002 *National Security Strategy* insists that the United States "has long maintained the option of preemptive actions to counter a sufficient threat to our national security." The greater the threat, "the greater is the risk of inaction—and the more compelling the case for taking anticipatory action to defend ourselves, even if uncertainty remains as to the time and place of the enemy's attack. To forestall or prevent such hostile acts by our adversaries, the United States will, if necessary, act preemptively."[21] In the document's preamble George Bush insists that in the "new world we have entered, the only path to peace and security is the path of action." This means that "as a matter of common sense and self-defense," the United States will act against "emerging" threats "before they are fully formed."[22] The 2006 *National Security Strategy* reiterates that "[t]he place of preemption in our national security strategy remains the same."[23] Conceding that for centuries international jurists and legal scholars have "conditioned the legitimacy of preemption on the existence of an imminent threat," the 2002 *National Security Strategy* insists that the United States "must adapt the concept of imminent threat to the capabilities and objectives of today's adversaries." Rogue states and terrorists "do not seek to attack us using conventional means." Instead they rely on "acts of terror and, potentially, the use of weapons of mass destruction" that are easily concealed "and can be used without warning."[24]

The expansion of the doctrine of preemptive war beyond the zone of imminent threat was reaffirmed in an ironic way by the failure to find WMD or a reconstituted nuclear weapons program in Iraq. Senior administration officials had predicted widely and often that they existed and would be found—most dramatically in Secretary of State Colin Powell's speech to the UN Security Council on February 5, 2003. Powell, a career military man who had been chairman of the Joint Chiefs of Staff during the 1991 Gulf War, was the most popular and senior African American in American politics. His 1996 flirtation with a bid for the presidency had enabled the hard Right, whose grip on the Republican Party was tightening, to smoke him out as too moderate to win the nomination.

This known skeptic of the neoconservative architects of the Bush Doctrine laid his credibility on the line, deploying satellite images of supposed WMD programs and intelligence to establish that Iraq was developing a weapons program "in order to project power, to threaten, and to deliver chemical, biological and, if we let him, nuclear warheads."[25] The speech, modeled on UN ambassador Adlai Stevenson's famous use of damning surveillance photographs of Soviet missiles in Cuba before the same body forty years earlier, bolstered the administration's case. Officials lost few opportunities—including conjuring up images of mushroom clouds over American cities—to insinuate that the threat was indeed imminent. Eventually Colin Powell would admit that this was a "blot" on his record.[26]

Not so the rest of the administration. When it transpired that there were no WMD or nuclear programs in Iraq, the administration responded partly by insisting that theirs was a reasonable mistake inasmuch as the Clinton administration, Democrats on the Hill who saw the intelligence estimates, and America's allies had all been persuaded that the WMD and nuclear programs existed. But the administration was also quick to insist—even though this stood in tension with their blame-spreading stance—that President Bush and other senior administration officials had never claimed that the threat from Iraq was in fact imminent. They had used terms like *grave*, *gathering*, *serious*, and *mortal*, but the I-word had not been deployed.[27] The administration and its defenders quickly put the president's critics on the defensive by demanding proof that the term *imminent* had been used when in reality it had not been. The resulting squabbles about the extent to which imminence had and had not been implied in the administration's rhetoric—didn't *immediate* mean imminent?, etc.—obscured the more important reality: that the architects of the Bush Doctrine no longer regarded the imminence of threat as decisive. They had moved from expanding the definition of imminence in the *National Security Strategy*, based on claims about changed technologies of destruction and enemies with unprecedented motivations, to the position that imminent threats—however defined—are no longer needed to justify preemptive war.

If imminent threats are unnecessary to justify America's going to war, what is? In a fourth—and in some ways the most radical—departure from traditional U.S. and Republican orthodoxy, the Bush Doctrine envisages replacing oppressive dictatorships with democracies as sufficient to legitimate an American invasion. "The American people know my position," President Bush said of Iraq at a press conference at his Texas ranch in August of 2002, ". . . and that is that regime change is in the interest of the world."[28] The general principle was outlined in his preamble to the 2002 *National Security Strategy*, where Bush announced that "the United States will use this moment of opportunity to extend the benefits of freedom across the globe. We will actively work to bring the hope of democracy, development, free markets, and free trade to every corner of the world."[29] The 2006 *National Security Strategy* reiterates that stance: "To protect our Nation and honor our values, the United States seeks to extend freedom across the globe by leading an international effort to end tyranny and to promote effective democracy."[30]

As the administration came to rely more heavily on this rationale for the Iraq invasion, officials noted that the Clinton administration had also favored regime change in Iraq after 1998.[31] But the Clinton administration had never planned to install democracy in Iraq by deploying American forces. A reluctant President Clinton was cajoled into signing the Iraq Liberation Act of 1998 by Republicans in Congress and a campaign mounted by neoconservative think tanks and the Iraqi National Congress (INC)—an expatriate group based in Britain and the United States.[32] The legislation was meant to fund the Iraqi insurgency to the tune of $97 million, but the State Department—

skeptical of the effectiveness of the INC—had disbursed no more than $8 million of it by the time President Clinton left office.[33] This was a far cry from the forcible regime change, not only in Iraq but in Iran, Syria, Libya, and Saudi Arabia, that is frankly advocated by neoconservatives like David Frum and Richard Perle.[34]

Now there is a venerable American tradition of promoting democracy internationally. In 1917 Woodrow Wilson famously declared that the world "must be made safe for democracy."[35] Thirty years later President Truman insisted that "it must be the policy of the United States to support free peoples who are resisting subjugation by armed minorities or outside pressures."[36] Some of the rhetoric in the 2002 *National Security Strategy* echoes these sentiments. It is quite a stretch, however, from "encouraging free and open societies on every continent" or even creating "a balance of power that favors human freedom," as the document puts it,[37] to achieving regime change through military invasion. Yet the administration kept up a drumbeat of insistence from the beginning that forcible regime change was justified on the grounds that Saddam Hussein was a brutal dictator who had attacked his neighbors and gassed 300,000 Iraqi Kurds. The claim was also made repeatedly that regime change in Iraq would make America and the world safer, or, as President Bush put it in his January 2004 State of the Union, "For all who love freedom and peace, the world without Saddam Hussein's regime is a better and safer place."[38] This rationale did not wear well as Al Qaeda terrorists flowed into Iraq from North Africa and the Middle East. Journalists and other citizens from "coalition of the willing" countries were kidnapped and executed. Spain and Britain became targets of retaliatory terrorist bombings in 2004 and 2005—with the Italians warned that they would be next.

With the WMD war rationale defunct by the start of 2005,[39] all that remained of the administration's assorted war aims was the inherent desirability of replacing a brutal dictatorship with a democracy. Without the invasion, as President Bush put it in his 2004 State of the Union, "Iraq's torture chambers would still be filled with victims— terrified and innocent. The killing fields of Iraq, where hundreds of thousands of men, women and children vanished into the sands, would still be known only to the killers."[40] The contrast with candidate Bush's stance in his race against Al Gore in the 2000 election could not be starker. "He believes in nation building," said Bush in the first presidential debate. "I believe we're overextended in too many places."[41] Bush repeated this in the second debate, adding: "I'm going to be judicious as to how to use the military. It needs to be in our vital interest, the mission needs to be clear, and the exit strategy obvious."[42]

Whether and to what extent bringing democracy to Iraq had been a disingenuous war aim at the start continues to be debated, but walking away from it became increasingly difficult as the other war aims fell apart. And this despite the reality that democratic nation building was proving vastly more difficult than the administration had expected, with civic order, infrastructure, and even clean water and regular electricity supply a considerable distance from being restored by mid-2006—not to mention the fact that by the 2006 U.S. midterm elections, the number of U.S. military killed in Iraq would exceed that of the civilians killed in the 9/11 attacks.[43]

The regime change rationale created divisions in the

conservative movement—divisions that would likely esca-
late if the war dragged on without positive resolution.[44] But
it also created divisions on the left, with some trenchant
critics of all things Republican supporting the war. Christopher Hitchens backed the invasion in a series of articles in
Slate magazine, as did Paul Berman in the *New Republic* and
his book *Terror and Liberalism*.[45] As time wore on, many
Democrats found themselves torn between wanting to see
a war they had opposed succeed in bringing democracy to
Iraq and wanting to see the administration punished for its
reckless policies.

The architects of the Bush Doctrine made it clear, fifth,
that there was no possibility of neutrality in the coming
war on terror. The week after the 9/11 attacks, the president invoked divine authority on behalf of this stance.
"Freedom and fear, justice and cruelty, have always been
at war," he noted, "and we know that God is not neutral
between them."[46] As the invasion of Afghanistan began in
October, the president was unequivocal that "every nation
has a choice to make. In this conflict, there is no neutral
ground."[47] The following month he elaborated with the
claim that the United States was embarking on a war "to
save civilization itself." We "did not seek it, but we will
fight it and we will prevail," he said—leaving no doubt
that others must join. "Over time it's going to be important for nations to know they will be held accountable
for inactivity," Bush continued. "You're either with us or
against us in the fight against terror."[48] Later that month, at
a Warsaw conference on combating terrorism, the president went further, insisting that the war on terror "requires
an international coalition of unprecedented scope and cooperation" involving "sustained actions of many nations

against the network of terrorist cells and bases and funding." He warned that he would shortly "put every nation
on notice" at the UN "that these duties involve more than
sympathy or words. No nation can be neutral in this conflict, because no civilized nation can be secure in a world
threatened by terror."[49] The administration remained unequivocal on this in the 2006 *National Security Strategy*: "All
free nations have a responsibility to stand together for freedom because all free nations share an interest in freedom's
advance."[50] Contrast this with candidate Bush's insistence in
October 2000 that "one way for us to end up being viewed
as the ugly American is for us to go around the world saying, we do it this way, so should you."[51]

The Bush Doctrine in effect declares null and void the
international law on neutrality that stretches back to the
nineteenth century and was codified in the Hague Convention of 1907—to which the United States is a signa-
tory.[52] The neutrality asserted by countries like Ireland, Swe-
den, Switzerland, and Liechtenstein in World War II (not to
mention that of the United States until 1941 as provided
for in the Neutrality Act of 1935),[53] and the less formal
neutrality of the nonaligned nations during the Cold War,
would not be acceptable in the coming war on terror.
Some American politicians were hostile to neutrality during the Cold War. President Eisenhower's secretary of state
John Foster Dulles was famous for his view that neutrals
were worse than communists.[54] But not until the George
W. Bush administration did it become the announced policy of the U.S. government to repudiate the international
law of neutrality. At stake here was a good deal more than
rechristening french fries as "freedom fries" in cafeterias on
Capitol Hill.[55] Any advantages that might accrue from

limiting escalation of conflicts, and the existence of buffer zones and back channels, would be unavailable in the new war on terror.

Lest anyone suppose that this was mere heady talk in the immediate aftermath of 9/11, the administration has consistently repeated its "no neutral ground" position since that time. "No nation can be neutral in the struggle between civilization and chaos," Mr. Bush said before the American Legion's national convention in St. Louis, in November of 2003. "Every nation that stands on the side of freedom and the value of human life must condemn terror and act against the few who destroy the hopes of the many."[56] Following the attacks on Madrid's train networks in March of 2004, President Bush reiterated that "there can be no separate peace with the terrorist enemy." He remained adamant that "there is no neutral ground—no neutral ground—in the fight between civilization and terror, because there is no neutral ground between good and evil, freedom and slavery, and life and death." It is impossible to opt out, because the war on terror is "not a figure of speech." It is the "inescapable calling of our generation."[57]

A final distinctive feature of the Bush Doctrine is that it envisages a condition of permanent war. President Bush put it mildly in his introduction to the 2002 *National Security Strategy* when he said that the "war against terrorists of global reach is a global enterprise of uncertain duration."[58] It is in the nature of a war against "terror," as distinct from a particular regime, enemy, or even doctrine, that there is never going to be a final victory. There will always be those who see the spread of *pax Americana* contemplated in the Bush Doctrine as threatening and humiliating—not least because of the nonnegotiable way in which it has been forced on the whole world.

There will be no one, in the war on terror, with whom to sign an armistice—let alone from whom to extract a surrender. Particular terrorist organizations like the Bader-Meinhof group might melt away. "Rogue" states might change their tune and their actions from time to time, as Libya has done. The African National Congress or the Irish Republican Army might unilaterally suspend their armed struggles for one reason or another. But terrorism can no more be stamped out than can crime, and if the response to it is war, it will therefore be a permanent war. There will always be new violent extrastate groups, and new cells of older groups, whose members lack the resources or the inclination to pursue their agendas without recourse to violence. There will invariably be those who will find it profitable or rewarding for other reasons to support them. Indeed, in November 2001 President Bush identified terrorists as operating in sixty countries.[59] The proliferation of cheap, small weapons of enormous destructive power makes it unimaginable that terrorism can be stamped out for all time. Administration spokesmen acknowledge this when they say, as they invariably do, that the question is not whether we will be attacked again but when.[60] The notion that governments can achieve monopolies over coercive force that is perceived as legitimate is a conceit that naive generals and politicians share with Weberian sociologists.[61] The architects of the Bush Doctrine might have been shortsighted about many things, but they appear not to harbor illusions about this.

It will become plain from the following chapters that

the Bush Doctrine is unsustainable. Policies of unilateralism and preemptive war on a global scale make vast demands on the U.S. Treasury. Pursuing them into the indefinite future is fiscally unthinkable. In addition to their crippling economic cost, these policies are not sustainable politically at home or abroad. The demands on military personnel would mean bringing back the draft, a political third rail that not even the Bush administration is willing to contemplate touching. Downgrading traditional alliances in favor of "coalitions of the willing" will be counterproductive for the United States and will invite opportunism from adversaries. Continuing to ride roughshod over international law and institutions will also be self-defeating, placing impossible demands on American diplomacy. Fostering democracy around the world is a worthy and prudent American goal, but the Bush Doctrine undermines it. Subversive of the legitimacy on which democracies depend, it is, as we will see, more likely to foster insurgencies and anti-American nationalism than fledgling democracies.

If the Bush Doctrine is unsustainable, why the need for an alternative? Won't it simply collapse on its pile of contradictions and non sequiturs? By 2006 it was obvious that the administration's approach was failing to deal with the threats and realities of nuclear proliferation in North Korea, India, Pakistan, and Iran, and it was being forced to canvass alternative possibilities. Without acknowledging this explicitly, administration officials began shifting emphasis. Instead of insisting on the obsolescence of traditional American doctrines of deterrence and containment, they were leaning more often on less strident formulations—such as that these doctrines must be augmented by the Bush Doctrine.

But there's the rub. Saying that we need to augment traditional doctrines of containment and deterrence with the Bush Doctrine is like saying that we need to augment traditional methods of putting out fires with water by pouring gasoline on them. Containment and deterrence have always depended for their effectiveness on principled and predictable American action on the world stage, on nurturing alliances with traditional allies, and on support for—and judicious use of—international institutions. The new challenges we face owing to transnational terrorist groups and weak states make these things more important, not less important. Yet the Bush administration has squandered much of America's moral capital, strained traditional alliances in unprecedented ways with its haphazard unilateralism, and weakened vital international institutions. Harmful as its policies have been to America's interests and security, it would be naive to suppose that a great deal more damage cannot be done before the Bush Doctrine finds its way into the trash can of history. Hence the urgent need for the alternative propounded here.

4   Containment for Democracy

A government's obligation to protect its citizens from violent attack lies at the core of every plausible national security doctrine. This means being ready to respond effectively to attacks, and it legitimates the use of preemptive force when such attacks are imminent. Demanding as these injunctions might often be to meet, that they should be met is uncontroversial in U.S. historical practice, international law, and common sense. No government would be elected if it failed to embrace them, and none should expect to survive for long if the electorate comes to believe it incompetent to meet them. These are the nonnegotiable features of national security policy. Allies and adversaries must accept them, and anyone seeking to develop a plausible national security doctrine must address them.

Things become more controversial once we focus on how best to be prepared for actual and imminent attacks, and on what the approach should be to threats and potential threats that are less than imminent. It is on these subjects that America must part company with the Bush Doctrine. We must revisit the national security doctrines that have served us well in the past, adapting them to the changed reality we now confront.

The doctrine of containment was originally developed by George Kennan during the late 1940s in response to the emerging Soviet threat. Keenly aware of the price the Allies had paid for their halting response to Hitler during the 1930s and distrustful of Stalin's expansionist agenda for the USSR, Kennan persuaded President Truman and his foreign policy establishment that there was a viable third way between appeasement and the chimerical aspiration to achieve U.S. control over the global security environment. Containment was a complex doctrine that took on various forms, not all of which garnered Kennan's approval.[1] There are, moreover, major differences between the Soviet threat faced during the Cold War and the threats and potential threats that America confronts today. Nonetheless, Kennan's outlook and reasoning supply better tools for thinking about how to confront them than either the Bush Doctrine or anything that has been put forward by its critics.

Containment's central project was a quest for national security that required neither pursuit nor maintenance of worldwide military supremacy. It rested on what John Lewis Gaddis points out was a particularist understanding of U.S. security interests. "What was required was not to remake the world in the image of the United States, but simply to preserve its diversity against attempts to remake it in the image of others."[2] For centuries it has been a staple of republican political theory that empires invariably become overextended and collapse.[3] Kennan and the other architects of containment built on this intellectual legacy, however unwittingly. Indeed, part of their motivation was the conviction that "patient but firm and vigilant containment of Russian expansive tendencies" would eventually be rewarded by Soviet implosion as *its* imperial ambitions became unsustainable.[4] The objective was to build "an international order made up of independent centers of power, in which nations subject to Soviet pressure would have both the means and the will to resist it themselves."[5] Hence Kennan's strong support for the Marshall Plan to ensure the rapid reconstitution of Europe, and his refusal to conflate the Soviet threat with international communism. The existence of competition within the communist world struck him as a useful constraint on Soviet expansionism. Unlike John Foster Dulles, who pushed for worldwide resistance to the International Communist Movement, Kennan saw the principal threat to the United States as the possibility of Soviet hegemony—not communism as such.[6] The goal was to foster "a heretical drifting-away process on the part of the satellite states." However weak they might be in the short run, he argued, "grounds do exist for heretical schisms. We can contribute to the widening of these rifts without assuming responsibility. And when the final breaks occur, we would not be directly involved in engaging Soviet prestige; the quarrel would be between the Kremlin and the Communist Reformation."[7]

Kennan built containment around a basic distinction between vital and peripheral interests. War was justifiable when a vital interest was threatened, though it should always be the strategy of last resort. Overwhelming force would be needed, with potentially catastrophic consequences in the nuclear era. War almost never made sense for the defense of peripheral interests on Kennan's account. Fighting low-grade "cheap" wars over issues or territories not vital to America's survival might be tempting, particularly if it appeared that points could be scored against the Soviets. The great danger, as the United States would learn to its cost in Indochina, was that, peripheral as the interest in question might be to the United States, it would often be vital to the local adversaries for whom everything would be at stake. They would therefore inevitably ratchet things up, forcing the United States to employ disproportionate—and most likely unsustainable—force. The Kennedy administration initially backed into Vietnam with thirty-five hundred troops, thought by McGeorge Bundy to be "good medicine." Yet the United States was forced eventually to give up with half a million committed troops and fifty-eight thousand American dead—a textbook illustration of Kennan's point.[8]

Waging such wars will inevitably cast the United States in the role of the imperialist. Local populations will rally around anti-American ideologies. Support for the war at home will just as inevitably erode as the casualties and other costs mount, and more pressing priorities take center stage. Peripheral interests should therefore be pursued by means other than war: diplomacy, economic incentives, sanctions, and the use of multilateral and international institutions.

Kennan's commitment to containment was perhaps more strategic than principled, rooted in what he thought would work. It also reflected his recognition, as millions of soldiers were being demobilized after the war and military spending was being sharply cut, that national security would have to be assured on significantly reduced resources. Certainly the reasons Kennan typically advanced in support of containment were primarily strategic, geared to hemming in the USSR at minimal cost to the United States. Yet it is essential to see that although containment is indeed in America's strategic interest, it can and should be defended as the best available principled basis for U.S. national security policy. This is inherently important, but it is also a political imperative because principled arguments are needed to sustain support for any national security policy over time. People like to act in what they think are their interests, to be sure, but it is also important to them to believe that the cause they are being asked to support is morally right.

Kennan's objective, to prevent hostile powers from achieving dominance while eschewing any agenda for American global supremacy, does indeed provide a morally appealing strategic basis for securing America as a democracy into the future. Democracy has been intimately linked to the project of undermining domination at least since Machiavelli said in the early sixteenth century that the common people should be the guardians of freedom because—unlike the aristocracy, whose desire is to dominate— their desire is not to be dominated.[9] True, democracy carries with it the danger of majority tyranny, against which possibility the American founders designed various institutional constraints, but history has proved Machiavelli right. Democracies do better at preserving freedom and preventing domination than do nondemocracies, supporting the adage that the one thing worse than majority tyranny is minority tyranny. Particularly since modern political science has taught us to be skeptical that majority rule embodies anything that can coherently be described as a "general will," it is democracy's intrinsic antipathy to domination that supplies its moral legitimacy. This is most importantly true in authoritarian settings, where the experience of domination leads opposition groups to demand democracy and to fight for it.[10] For the United States to be committed to undermining domination in the world without seeking to establish its own supremacy is to affirm a principle that flows naturally out of its democratic raison d'être, and it can appeal to those who harbor democratic inclinations everywhere.

Critics of the Bush Doctrine were caught wrong-footed by the Bush administration's claim that it is *they* who are abolishing tyranny and spreading democracy around the world. After all, it is Democrats who have traditionally pushed for America to foster democracy abroad, whereas Republicans have tended to support regimes deemed favorable to short-run American interests, as when the Eisenhower administration helped overthrow Iran's democracy in 1953 and install the shah, and otherwise to look skeptically on foreign adventures. The ascent of neoconservative thinking in the Bush administration scrambled that reality. Congressional Democrats could do little but join the standing ovation when the president opened his 2005 State of the Union by congratulating the freshly elected members for the privilege they shared with the elected leaders of Afghanistan and Iraq, among others.[11] Bush might have lost conservatives like Patrick Buchanan and Francis Fukuyama,[12] but he seemed to have pulled the rug out from under the traditional opposition.

Critics of the Bush administration should not have been wrong-footed so quickly by this improbable and precarious agenda. Just because of democracy's intimate association with resistance to tyranny and domination, attempts to ram it down people's throats at the point of a gun will likely be seen as hypocritical and self-serving. It is scarcely surprising, in this regard, that the Afghan and Iraqi elections have not enabled their governments, which could not survive a week without American military protection, to shed the albatross of being U.S. puppet regimes. The idea behind containment is to refuse to be bullied, while at the same time declining to become a bully. The

Bush Doctrine's moral bankruptcy inheres in its lack of the resources for avoiding that trap. Its proponents fail to realize that democracy has rarely been successfully imposed by a conquering power. As John Stuart Mill noted a century and a half ago, if democracy is imposed on a country where there is insufficient indigenous support to achieve it, the strong likelihood is that it will collapse again into tyranny.[13]

When democracy has been successfully imposed, as in West Germany and Japan after World War II, this was in the highly unusual circumstance where large majorities of both the domestic populations and the rest of the democratic world accepted the legitimacy of the imposition following defeats that the German and Japanese dictatorships had brought upon their own populations by attacking the Allied powers. Since democracy depends for its legitimacy on widespread acceptance, this is no trivial condition. The prospects for meeting it have never been strong in Iraq, though they were arguably better in the aftermath of the 1991 Gulf War than when regime change was actually attempted in the spring of 2003. The earlier conflict had been the undeniable consequence of unprovoked Iraqi aggression against Kuwait, and the large coalition assembled by the first President Bush and sanctified by the UN enjoyed great international legitimacy. That coalition of forces would have been considerably better placed to bring about democratic regime change than the second President Bush's coalition "of the willing" that invaded in flat defiance of much democratic world opinion in an action that was seen by most Iraqis as an opportunistic attack.[14]

In the event the first President Bush stopped short of

regime change partly because he knew that this would have fractured his international coalition, and partly because then chairman of the Joint Chiefs Colin Powell and then secretary of defense Dick Cheney were convinced that pacifying postwar Iraq and building a democracy there would be too costly.[15] As the West German and Japanese examples underscore, installing democracy in a defeated country takes many years of occupation and massive economic investment while new institutions and attitudes take hold and the economy revives enough to give the fledgling regime a fighting chance.[16] Unless invading powers are going to be in a position to make that kind of investment, containment will be the better strategy—supplemented, when feasible, by refusal to underwrite the dictatorship and support for the country's indigenous democratic opposition. Containment's anti-imperial stance is more apt to be seen as legitimate at home and abroad, and, partly for that reason, is more likely to work.

Contrast this defense of containment in the service of democracy with Francis Fukuyama's recent critique of the Bush Doctrine.[17] Once a neoconservative who urged forcible regime change in Iraq on the Clinton administration in 1998,[18] Fukuyama has now abandoned the cause partly because of the illegitimacy that attaches to trying to impose democratic regime change with coalitions of the willing. But Fukuyama now argues instead for a kind of "multi-multilateralism" in which the United States should "forum shop" for the "appropriate instrument" to facilitate American strategic goals. Fukuyama cites as an example the Clinton administration's use of NATO to justify intervening in the Kosovo conflict, when the Russian veto in the

Security Council foreclosed the possibility of UN action. NATO, he tells us, "provided legitimacy for military intervention in a way that the United Nations could not."[19]

But despite Fukuyama's high hopes for NATO, "which could get a second wind as a security organization in the wake of the collapse of the drive toward a European constitution,"[20] the Kosovo intervention is scarcely a model for international action to promote democracy. For one thing, NATO is a defensive alliance. Since no member nation was attacked or threatened with attack, the Kosovo military action violated its charter.[21] For another, Kosovo was a humanitarian intervention in the face of ongoing genocide, not an attempt at externally imposed regime change. It was this reality that mitigated the legitimacy problems, not the fact that NATO was the agent. Moreover, because the intervention in question was to protect Muslims, it lacked the ethnoreligious dimension that typically makes Western military action in the Middle East so problematic. If NATO were to act in a similar way when this was not the case, it would face considerably rougher sledding than it did in Kosovo.

The U.S. decision in early 2006 to turn operational control in Afghanistan over to NATO is in better keeping with the Charter—given the Afghan role in harboring Al Qaeda before and after the 9/11 attacks.[22] But the damage done to our international image by the Iraq war suggests that we should not anticipate much of an international legitimacy dividend. We have seen that during the 1950s, the authors of NSC-68 and the Truman Doctrine realized that preemptive war would cost the United States the moral high ground in the Cold War.[23] It has been enormously costly for the United States that the architects of

the Bush Doctrine failed to draw the analogous conclusion about the conflict with radical Islam.

The banner headline in *Le Monde* on September 12,
2001, read, "We are all Americans!"; countries across the
Muslim world condemned the Al Qaeda attacks; and there
were candlelight vigils for the fallen Americans even in
Tehran. Much water has flowed under the bridge since
then.[24] Five years of the Bush Doctrine have cost the
United States huge amounts of moral capital.[25] At a joint
press conference with Russian premier Vladimir Putin in
July of 2006, President Bush said, "I talked about my desire
to promote institutional change in parts of the world like
Iraq where there's a free press and free religion," expressing
the "hope that Russia would do the same thing." This invited the smug retort that "we, of course, would not want to
have a democracy like in Iraq."[26] It will take many years—
and the different policies I propose here—to restore America's moral authority on the subject of promoting democracy
around the world.

More generally, it is hard to see why Fukuyama imagines
that frankly opportunistic forum shopping will confer any
more legitimacy on U.S. military action than do frankly opportunistic coalitions of the willing. He believes that NATO
"has fewer legitimacy problems than the UN"[27] because it
is composed exclusively of democracies. But this begs the
questions: legitimacy in whose eyes, and for what purpose?
Where the motives for American action are overwhelm-
ingly suspect in the eyes of the domestic population of the
targeted country—as they were in Iraq in 2003—and no
NATO country is threatened with attack, it is difficult to
believe that there is more than a fig leaf to be gained by
NATO action. It will often be impossible to achieve the

kind of legitimacy that external intervention in the service of democratic regime change requires. In that case, the only feasible option is to support indigenous democratic forces and to withhold support from their authoritarian opponents. Like so many of the neoconservatives from whom he now seeks to distance himself, Fukuyama is tone-deaf to the ways in which the muscular worldwide assertion of American values is perceived by others. Containment avoids these difficulties by dint of its inherent anti-imperialism.

Indeed, containment is more behavioral than ideological in that its focus is on what potential adversaries do internationally rather than on their internal political arrangements or the beliefs of their leaders. Political theorists might discern in this an element of a stripped-down "political, not metaphysical" disposition, inasmuch as containment seeks a basis for interacting with others that does not depend on persuading them of the validity of your beliefs or the folly of theirs.[28] In Kennan's case this was born of the conviction that arguing with Soviet leaders about the merits of international issues was a waste of time since they could never be persuaded of the values and commitments of America's political leaders.[29] He thought the Soviets would, nonetheless, respond to the logic implicit in containment even if they were unwilling or unable to acknowledge that they were doing so. He thought this supplied the best basis for dealing with them.

However true this might have been of Soviet leaders during the Cold War, it seems even more obviously so of adversaries whose beliefs are sharply at odds with those of most Americans, and who lack any history of democratic politics. Seeking to convert them to our worldview seems, at best, naive. The fusion of communism and anti-American nationalism proved to be a potent mixture in Indochina and much of Africa and Latin America during the Cold War. There is every reason to expect the fusion of Islam and anti-American nationalism to be just as potent. The Arab world's reaction to the American invasion of Iraq vindicates that expectation.

Just as the Vietnam conflict solidified anti-Americanism in Southeast Asia, so the 2003 Iraq invasion has done it across the Middle East. The Bush administration has played into this dynamic, contributing to the "clash-of-civilizations" construction of what is at stake.[30] In the aftermath of 9/11 and in the 2002 *National Security Strategy* they were careful to avoid targeting Islam as such. But they also insisted that the war on terror is a war on people who hate "freedom" and hate us for who we are.[31] In a series of speeches in late 2005, President Bush began explicitly connecting the war on terror to variants of radical and militant Islam.[32] In this he was genuflecting in the direction of neoconservatives like David Frum and Richard Perle, who have long insisted that militant Islam is the principal cause of terrorism, that it is widely endorsed across the Muslim world and among Muslim minorities in the West, and that its goal is to "overthrow our civilization and remake the nations of the West into Islamic societies, imposing on the whole world its religion and its law."[33]

This analysis defies most expert opinion, which recognizes that since 1980 more terrorism, including suicide bombing, has been perpetrated by secular groups than by religious fundamentalists,[34] and that even Islamic terrorist leaders like bin Laden see themselves as engaged in a "defensive jihad" in response to American policies in the

Middle East, rather than an "offensive jihad" geared to the global spread of Islam.[35] Feeding the idea of a clash of civilizations is as self-defeating with respect to Islam as Kennan thought it was with respect to international communism.

Unnecessary anti-Americanism in the Middle East has been compounded by American saber rattling against Iran that started with President Bush's "Axis of Evil" speech in 2002, to the amazement of many in the Iranian government. Iran had been cooperating with the American action in Afghanistan and saw the invasion as an opportunity to put Iranian-American relations on a new footing. Hostile to both Al Qaeda and the Taliban government of Mullah Omar, they saw the U.S.-supported Northern Alliance as preferable.

From the perspective of containment, it is vital to support competition for power within potentially hostile regimes as well as competition among them. The Bush administration squandered opportunities on both fronts. Lumping Iran together with Iraq in the speech played into the hands of forces interested in building an anti-American pan-Shiite—if not pan-Muslim—movement. The traditional ethnic and national rivalries between Iraqi and Iranian Shiites have faded into the background as Iranian and Iraqi Shiites have cooperated in the face of a common enemy. As one journalist noted to me in early 2006, if one called to reserve a hotel room in southern Iraq, the phone was as likely to be answered in Persian as in Arabic. It is small wonder that the 2006 Chatham House report on Iran concludes that it has been "the chief beneficiary of the war on terror in the Middle East."[36]

Iran was what former NSC official Kenneth Pollack

describes as "roadkill." Senior Bush officials told him that it was tossed into the 2002 State of the Union at the last minute as a prop by speechwriters who had "come up with this great line, and needed a third country to make up the 'Axis.' "[37] Perhaps some in the administration had other agendas. Despite Iran's ongoing cooperation in Afghanistan, in early January of 2002 Israel intercepted a ship carrying Iranian weapons and explosives in the Red Sea. There is some debate over whether they were destined for the Palestinian Authority in violation of its agreements with Israel, as Israeli intelligence contended.[38] But the fact of their apprehension decisively weakened the hand of officials who were urging that Iran be kept out of the speech on the grounds that it had an incipient democratic movement that should be encouraged.[39]

The decision to include Iran exhibited frighteningly little grasp of Iranian politics, in which conservative mullahs had been on the defensive since the reformist Mohammad Khatami's election to the presidency in 1997. There were good reasons for thinking their influence was in decline. Khatami was reelected in June of 2001.[40] Iran is a country with a decidedly pro-Western young population.[41] Its politics is marked by competing power centers and intense political factionalism. Apart from the supreme leader, Ayatollah Ali Khamenei, foreign policy is influenced by the elected president, the National Security Council, the Council of Guardians, and the Expediency Council. This last was created in 1989 to resolve interagency disputes—by its very existence an illustration of the pluralization of politics within the regime.[42] Even in 2006 there was evidence of competition within the regime over its nuclear policy. In June of 2006 Khamenei created a new Strategic Council for Foreign Relations, to which he appointed political figures who had been associated with the reformist Khatami era. This suggested an agenda to diminish, or at least counterbalance, hard-line President Mahmoud Ahmadinejad's rogue pronouncements on international affairs.[43]

Iran's parliament is divided among fiercely competing factions ranging from conservative forces, for whom any approach to the "great Satan" amounts to treason, to large numbers of reformers who openly advocate restoration of relations with the United States. But the latter lost control of parliament to the conservatives in 2004, and their leaders have been forced to acknowledge that Iran would be in an exceedingly weak position if it proposed talks at the height of American influence in the region.[44] With U.S. forces stationed in Afghanistan to the east, in Iraq to the west, and in the Persian Gulf to the south, how could a siege mentality *not* emerge? Not only was the country literally surrounded by forces of an openly hostile American government, but Iran's regional influence in Persian-speaking Afghanistan and Tajikistan was also curtailed.[45] It would be as if the Soviet Union had occupied Canada and Mexico at the height of the Cold War, and had its fleet anchored off Cuba.

Containment rises to the level of quarantine when there is no alternative, but part of Kennan's wisdom lay in advocating strategies to prevent things from getting to that point. Promoting competition among potential adversaries and avoiding policies that foster siege mentalities are prominent among them. Proponents of the Bush Doctrine ignored these imperatives partly to rally jingoism in the face of waning enthusiasm for the Iraq war at home, and partly, perhaps, because they have come to believe their own rhetoric about appeasement. This is a dangerous folly.

In 2003, supporters of the George W. Bush administration's Iraq policy lambasted their critics with the "appeasement" label when those critics called for more time for weapons inspectors and beefing up the sanctions. These attacks were fortified by the haunting specter of Neville Chamberlain at Munich.[46] As Republican Senator Ted Stevens of Alaska said on the Senate floor: "I vividly remember watching the world appease Hitler while he pursued an aggressive military policy aimed at dominating the world. . . . I see the next Hitler in Saddam Hussein." Two days before the invasion President Bush elaborated: "In the 20th century some chose to appease murderous dictators whose threats were allowed to grow into genocide and global war. In this century when evil men plot chemical, biological and nuclear terror, a policy of appeasement could bring destruction of a kind never before seen on this earth."[47]

Supposing, perhaps, that the implied comparison between George W. Bush and Winston Churchill would collapse of its own weight, Democrats never seriously engaged the appeasement charge. The obvious answer—though it never became part of the debate—was to invoke the doctrine of containment. Because it is geared to stopping those who seek domination, containment lives at irreconcilable odds with appeasement.

The early Allied response to Nazi Germany is usually held out as the classic illustration of appeasement's folly, as indeed it was. It bears on the discussion of containment in the face of modern terrorism inasmuch as Kennan himself speculated that Hitler, with his messianic commitment to realizing his agenda for the Third Reich on a strict timetable, might not have been containable.[48] What makes terrorism more and less containable is taken up in chapter 5. With respect to Hitler, we will never know what would have happened had his initial expansionist adventures brought forth an Allied response akin to that called forth by Saddam Hussein's invasion of Kuwait in August of 1990. In any event, the defense of containment is not that it will always work, but rather that it should always be attempted. When it fails, the logic of the doctrine implies ratcheting up in the face of defiance, not ratcheting down. Failures to contain never mean that aggression should be tolerated. You do what is needed to stop the bully without becoming a bully, but you must do what *is* needed to stop the bully. Containment is philosophically reactive, but it is strategically proactive when necessary.

Ironically, U.S. policy toward Iraq had been a model of successful containment since 1991—with the ignoble exception of our mixed signals toward, and eventual betrayal of, the democratic insurgency that erupted in southern Iraq in the wake of the Iraqi army's expulsion from Kuwait. The disciplined use of only sufficient force to expel Iraqi forces from Kuwait, the destruction of Saddam Hussein's WMD programs at the end of the war, the exclusion of his air force from no-fly zones in the Kurdish north and Shiite south all combined to ensure that Iraq posed no threat to any country—let alone to the United States. Moreover, the containment regime that was in place prior to March of 2003 enjoyed the international legitimacy that came with the imprimatur of the UN Security Council, and it was sustained at comparatively low military and economic cost to the United States.

In July of 2003 Deputy Secretary of Defense Paul Wolfowitz had griped to Congress that it had cost the United States some $30 billion "to maintain the so-called containment of Saddam Hussein for the last 12 years."[49] The irony is that the first three years after the March 2003 invasion came in at a price tag significantly in excess of ten times that amount,[50] with hundreds of billions more obviously still to come. Scholarly estimates put the eventual cost of the war possibly as high as $1.6 trillion.[51] Some have suggested that containment of Iraq would have become increasingly costly, especially if long-term hostility to the United States had persisted in the country and the region.[52] Perhaps so, but the reality is that the United States is going to face the costs of an extensive containment regime in the Middle East *in addition to* the huge cost of the Iraq war.

Containment in support of democracy does not rule out military alliances, but it implies that they should be geared in the first instance to preserving America as a democracy and then to the protection of other democracies. This priority does not rest on the supposition that American lives are more valuable than other lives, or that American democracy is more important than democracy elsewhere (though my argument will be attractive to people who believe those things). Rather, it reflects the reality that no government will long be in a position to protect others or to foster democracy elsewhere unless it can protect its own people and preserve its country as a democracy.

In this the imperative to secure American democracy

first is analogous to John Locke's injunction that each individual strive to preserve mankind to the extent that this is compatible with his or her self-preservation. This did not mean, for Locke, that a given person's self-interest was more important than the interests of others. On the contrary, Locke's signature and revolutionary view was that we are all equal in God's eyes. It is simply a matter of who has primary responsibility for what.[53] Despite containment's particularism, it is thus compatible with a cosmopolitan commitment to democracy that would suggest securing French democracy first as a French national security priority, securing South African democracy first as a South African national security priority, and so on.

Military cooperation with nondemocratic regimes may sometimes be unavoidable for securing American democracy, but this involves substantial risks and it threatens to erode the principled basis on which containment's legitimacy rests. As a result, it makes sense in dire circumstances only. For instance, 9/11 made it clear that apprehending the Al Qaeda leadership and dismantling its Afghan training camps was an absolute priority for American national security. Because the Taliban regime refused to cooperate in this endeavor, an invasion was needed. This, in turn, meant not only relying on Iran, as already discussed, but also cooperating with Pervez Musharraf of Pakistan—who had come to power in a military coup in October 1999. In this circumstance, cooperating with Musharraf was akin to cooperating with Stalin to defeat Hitler—a second-best choice, to be sure, but nonetheless a defensible one. Such cooperation should be accompanied by pressure on the regime in question to democratize, and in any case it should cease once the imperative that made it necessary has been achieved.[54]

Bilateral military alliances and collective defense agreements with other democracies will sometimes make sense. They are not obligatory, however. Often they will be too costly when peripheral interests are at stake, so that the better course will be to pursue networks of multilateral democratic alliances that can both increase security and diffuse the costs of enforcing it. When such alliances are entered into, they should be limited to mutual defense as NATO is. Should democratic allies become involved in aggressive wars and other forms of conquest, supporting them will erode America's legitimacy in the world and frustrate the protection of its vital strategic interests. America's international legitimacy depends on persuading others that we will not undertake or endorse imperial conquest, that we are about preventing domination—not fostering it.

The U.S. relationship with Israel is a case in point. Had our consistent policy been "We will underwrite your survival but not your conquests," our position in the Middle East would be vastly more tenable today. It would have meant supporting Israel in the 1967 Six-Day War and the 1973 Yom Kippur War, to be sure, but not in its 1982 invasion of Lebanon or the settlements in the West Bank and Gaza. Had we used our diplomatic and economic muscle—as we did with Britain and France during the Suez crisis of 1956—to prevent or undo these actions, the suspicion of U.S. motives across the Arab world would be much less widespread than it is. Instead, we have allowed U.S. aid to be fungible to the point that for all practical purposes it finances the settlements—feeding the perception that there is nothing Israel will do that the United States will not support.[55] Indeed, President Bush's declaration in April of 2004 that all parties must henceforth accept changed "realities on the ground" was the kind of about-face in U.S. policy that makes it all but impossible for us plausibly to claim evenhandedness.[56] If the battle for hearts and minds in the Middle East is between U.S. claims to be standing for democracy and freedom and bin Laden's insistence that our designs are partial and imperial, it is hard to imagine a more self-defeating stance for President Bush to have taken.[57] Who can be surprised that Gallup polls at the end of 2005 revealed only 15 percent of Palestinians approving of American leadership, 92 percent holding an unfavorable opinion of President Bush, and only 11 percent believing he had the capacity to help negotiate a fair peace treaty?[58] Containment has moral legitimacy precisely because it eschews domination. The Bush Doctrine, by contrast, is a raw assertion of American might. It is "premised on power," as President Bush's future deputy secretary of state, Robert Zoellick, put it in 2000.[59]

An additional source of containment's moral appeal derives from its affinity with the doctrine of just war, and particularly those parts of the doctrine that require force used always to be proportionate to the ends sought, and war always to be the strategy of last resort. Just war can never be wanton, and it must always be unavoidable.[60] We need not delve into the doctrine's ultimate basis, if it has one, to note that the policies flowing from containment do not contravene just war theory and might even be seen as embodying it. This is to say nothing of the fact that the ideas of proportionate force and war as the option of last resort are affirmed in much international law, lending additional legitimacy to the core ideas of containment. Kennan's claim that it offered a defensible third way between appeasement and the quest for supremacy was sound. Its intimate link to the project of preserving the United States as a democracy into the future, and its compatibility with widely accepted ethical systems, give it a principled basis that the Bush Doctrine manifestly lacks. But how realistic is containment in the post–9/11 era?

5 Containment's Realism

A good part of containment's appeal after World War II stemmed from its manifest realism. The nation's security had to be achieved with a reduced military and on diminished budgets. Necessity was the mother of invention. George Kennan offered a hard-nosed way of ordering threats that took account of postwar realities. Worldwide U.S. hegemony was not needed to protect vital American interests. Adversaries who could be neither vanquished nor won over could be managed. Competition among them would diffuse the threats they posed, and, as they came to see that the United States harbored no plan to attack them, tensions need not spiral out of control. Indeed, the threats might diminish. The duplicity and cynicism of Soviet leaders could not be discounted, to be sure, but there were good reasons to suppose that their imperial designs would be a source of their undoing.

The macroeconomic and global security environments were strikingly different after the Cold War. The Soviet implosion and the massive 1990s economic boom in the West combined to render the United States peerless as the world's economic dynamo and lone military superpower. Despite military cutbacks during the Clinton years, by the time George W. Bush came into office in January of 2001 U.S. military spending exceeded that of the world's ten next-largest military spenders combined.[1] Scarcity was not on many minds. The federal government was expected to be awash in budget surpluses as far as the eye could see—so much so that Federal Reserve chairman Alan Greenspan publicly fretted that the government might actually run out of debt.[2]

Containment had been a creature of the Cold War. It was far from clear that there was anyone left to contain after 1991, as former communist countries lined up to join NATO and the European Union, and China seemed bent, with the zeal of a convert, on soaking up foreign investment and joining the capitalist club. In 2001 President Bush appointed Donald Rumsfeld to downsize and reorganize the military—a task for which he seemed eminently well equipped. Rumsfeld had served as the youngest secretary of defense in American history during the Ford administration, but he had since spent more than two decades in business as a highly successful CEO of several large corporations. His agenda was to make use of modern flexible business practices to create a lighter, leaner, and more efficient military that would be supplemented by technological advances—notably satellite technology and accelerated investment in the "Star Wars" missile defense system initiated by President Reagan.[3]

The idea that the United States was sufficiently rich and powerful to buy invulnerable security from all possible threats took three major hits early in the new century. The attacks of 9/11 brought home to Americans what the British, French, Spanish, and Israelis had known for decades: that a sufficiently determined foe can wreak havoc with modest resources—regardless of one's military might. Then the Iraq war forced Americans to relearn what had been forgotten since Vietnam: that sustaining a war on the other side of the world against adversaries who believe they have everything at stake will quickly bog down, outstripping the projections of military planners.[4]

Any remaining doubts over whether the United States could continue such costly elective conflicts were put to rest by Hurricane Katrina, which devastated New Orleans in early September of 2005. The federal government had to commit $56 billion in aid by the second week of the disaster, as estimates of the eventual cost to the Treasury topped $200 billion.[5] Budget deficits were by then running in the $300 billion range, and the Iraq war costs—already in the hundreds of billions—showed no signs of abating.

Nor could expensive conflicts with others in the "Axis of Evil" be ruled out, as North Korean intransigence and the escalating saber rattling between the United States and Iran in mid-2006 made all too plain. This was to say nothing of unexpected new attacks, or conflicts that could erupt elsewhere in the world in which the United States might have to become involved. And then there was the gnawing specter of a fledgling Chinese superpower flexing its muscles in Asia, with the possibility that an expensive new arms race might erupt at any time.[6] By some accounts this has now begun.[7] Yet the Bush leadership remained allergic to any coherent ordering of dangers faced by the country or of proportionate responses to them. As Ron Suskind has documented, they remained wedded to Vice President Cheney's "one percent" doctrine: that threats intelligence professionals assigned even a 1 percent likelihood must be treated as certainties.[8]

In short, the reality was surfacing that the Bush Doctrine's predictable cost is staggering and without end. This is true not least because it has placed the United States on a permanent war footing. The "war on terror" is inherently open-ended, as we have seen. No politician will likely assume the risk of declaring it won, even though President Bush has committed—and recommitted—the nation to that goal. He has repeatedly insisted that America can accept nothing less than "total victory" in the war on terror, without ever explaining how this can be done or, indeed, what it might mean—even in principle.[9] What does seem clear is that the astronomical growth of military spending that is going to be required will make the military-industrial complex Dwight Eisenhower warned of in 1961 seem like child's play.[10]

The administration sought to limit the sticker shock of its military adventures in the short run by excluding Iraq and Afghanistan war costs from the budget, and spacing them out in a series of election cycle–sensitive requests for supplemental appropriations.[11] Yet by October of 2005 the Iraq war cost alone had passed the $250 billion mark.[12] Ongoing expenses were running at a monthly "burn rate" of about $5.9 billion—with an additional $1 billion a month for Afghanistan.[13] The United States was now spending more than the world's twenty next-largest military spenders combined.[14]

Nor was there much basis for confidence that the newly created Department of Homeland Security was doing its job. The administration's use of that reorganization to cut funding for domestic programs produced bureaucratic infighting and a drain of talent, the effects of which came to light with the inept response to Katrina.[15] Homeland Security allocations to the states were slashed in the wake of the disaster, making it plain that a major cost of the Bush Doctrine abroad was the inability to provide for adequate security at home.[16] This was especially troubling in view of arguments by such scholars as Robert Pape that enhanced homeland security is likely to be the most effective shield against terrorism.[17] The aftermath of the foiled plot to blow up airliners over the north Atlantic in August of 2006 made it plain that Pape is right. Yet, as one analyst noted in *Mother Jones*, delayed security upgrades for subway and commuter rail systems could be paid for by twenty days' worth of Iraq war spending. Missing explosives screening for all U.S. passenger airlines could be covered by ten days' worth. Overdue security upgrades for 361 American airports could be covered by four days' worth.[18] Katrina had shown how unprepared for catastrophic events the United States is, yet in 2006 the administration's budget reportedly cut funds to cities and states for infrastructure protection and first responders by more than a quarter.[19]

This is to say nothing of the looming military manpower crunch owing to the inability to draw down troops in Iraq and the dearth of recruitment for the National Guard—let alone the professional military.[20] Early in 2006 it was reported that officers, including West Point graduates, were leaving the military in record numbers at the first opportunity, forcing inordinate promotions and a concomitant reduction in the quality of the officer corps.[21] At best this implied added fiscal strain to make military service more appealing with an all-volunteer force. More likely it would eventually concretize the looming specter of a draft. The Bush Doctrine was playing out in a fiscal climate that increasingly resembled the late 1940s more than it did the late 1990s.

Moreover, the much-heralded regional "democratic domino effect" of the invasion had failed to materialize. In speeches during his second term President Bush was continuing to push the idea that benign democracy would spread like fire through the Middle East and beyond,[22] but it was increasingly clear that at best he was chasing an illusion over the horizon. By early 2006, promised elections had been postponed in Egypt. Those in the Palestinian Authority and Iran had produced governments strongly hostile to the United States, with Iran—emboldened by the demonstration of massive American weakness in Iraq—newly defiant about restarting its nuclear program. Any suggestion that a democratic domino effect wrought by the Bush Doctrine would permit the United States to reduce its costly military deployments in the region looked about as plausible as prewar predictions that Iraqi oil revenues would pay for the country's reconstruction.[23] If ever there was a time to rethink the abandonment of containment as the basis for U.S. national security, this was it.

The obvious place to start is containment's track record of great success in dealing with the Soviet Union, a departure from the policy of "rollback" that was contemplated in the second Truman and Eisenhower administrations—not to mention the urgings of preventive war from some in the military establishment.[24] A hostile nuclear superpower, committed to destruction of the political and economic systems of the West, was systematically hemmed into the sphere of influence it had consolidated by the 1950s. Despite major tensions over the four decades of Cold War that threatened to boil over into open conflict, superpower war was avoided without containment's ever collapsing into appeasement. The Cuban missile crisis made the Soviets realize that they risked Armageddon if they threatened vital American interests. Their attempts to wield influence in

Africa, the Middle East, and Latin America—areas of peripheral interest to the United States—were frustrated by various instruments of containment: diplomatic initiatives, economic sticks and carrots, and support for indigenous anticommunist forces and other surrogates.

Vietnam was the exception that proved the rule. The United States abandoned containment by waging what was expected to be a low-cost war in defense of a peripheral interest. The result was relentless escalation followed by ignoble retreat when the war's enormous human and economic cost destroyed support for it at home. For the most part, as with the Carter administration's response to the Soviet invasion of Afghanistan in 1979, the policy over peripheral interests was to find measures short of U.S. involvement in war to dissuade the Soviets from aggression, or, when this failed, to make their actions as costly to them as possible. In contrast to the scores of millions who died during the world wars, a potentially much worse superpower nuclear conflict was avoided without the West's ever having to capitulate.

But that was then, and this is now. Perhaps the post-9/11 threats are so different that containment is no longer equal to them. Proponents of the Bush Doctrine have extracted a great deal of mileage for their policies out of this view, though the precise nature of the changed threats is elusive. Various factors are frequently mentioned in commentary on the "war on terror." Sometimes the emphasis is on changes in technology and its proliferation—with the result that devastating low-cost attacks are easier to execute. Sometimes the focus is on the decentralized and transnational character of terrorist groups, or the messianic commitments of suicide attackers and those who send them. These are said to make them immune to containment, rational incentives, or meaningful negotiations. "Rogue" states are alleged to exhibit similar features. An additional concern is the proliferation of weak states. Their governments may be unable to control terrorist groups operating within their borders even if they want to.

These factors should be considered separately and soberly. All too often they are run together, creating a panicky fog through which it is easy to lose sight of the problem and viable approaches to it. Listen to President Bush's justification of his imminent invasion of Iraq in his 2003 State of the Union:

> Before September the 11th, many in the world believed that Saddam Hussein could be contained. But chemical agents, lethal viruses and shadowy terrorist networks are not easily contained. Imagine those 19 hijackers with other weapons and other plans—this time armed by Saddam Hussein. It would take one vial, one canister, one crate slipped into this country to bring a day of horror like none we have ever known. We will do everything in our power to make sure that that day never comes.[25]

President Bush is ambiguous, here, concerning whether it is Saddam Hussein, the chemical and biological weapons, or the terrorist networks that defy containment. In reality, some of the security challenges we face are not new and have been successfully managed in the past. Where they are new, the Bush Doctrine either fails to respond to them or makes them worse. There are no guarantees in life, to be sure, but the policies flowing from containment are a better bet for America's security. This becomes clearer if we sepa-rate the various claims President Bush conflates, and ex-amine them more closely.

New Technologies of Destruction

The Soviet collapse made vivid the danger that unemployed scientists, skilled at the creation of WMD, might find them-selves marketable to rogue regimes or terrorist groups. This, intensified by the specter of an international black market for lethal materials, poses obvious national security risks. The actual character of the threat is difficult to predict or calibrate, since there is a large array of nations and groups that might have either the ideology or the resources to ap-peal to someone with the relevant skills.

Despite beating the drum about this possibility, it is no-table that the Bush Doctrine offers no wisdom on how to deal with it. The administration's unilateralism is, if any-thing, an obstacle to the international cooperation and in-telligence sharing needed in the face of such a threat. We have to do what we can to limit the spread of WMD: use the available alliances and incentives to enforce nonprolif-eration agreements, invest in homeland security, work on antidotes to biological weapons, and increase protection of our own stockpiles. (One reason the Bush administration was so confident that Iraq had retained a biological weapons capability was that the United States had inad-vertently given it to them during the Iran-Iraq War).[26]

Advocates of the Bush Doctrine claim that contain-ment will not stop dangerous regimes from building or acquiring WMD. After all, Saddam Hussein expelled the UN weapons inspectors in 1998, and the Bush administration was right to insist that his compliance with weapons inspections in 2002 and early 2003 resulted from the buildup of U.S. and British troops on his borders. They might have been wrong about what he had achieved on the WMD front, but they were right that the old containment regime would not necessarily stop him from trying to rearm.

But this establishes nothing about the wisdom of the military buildup. The Bush administration boxed itself into the invasion by making the buildup unilateral. As a strategy to force Saddam's compliance with weapons inspections, this was a nonstarter. If, indeed, there was no other way to get the inspectors back into Iraq, and the WMD threat was judged too potentially serious to deal with by other means, the better course would have been to do as Bush senior had done: build up a meaningful international coalition *before* moving troops into the arena. Then troops of many nationalities could have rotated in and out—keeping up the pressure without allowing weather and the short timeline for maintaining the U.S. military buildup to drive events.

Now it might well have been impossible to generate the agreement needed for multilateral action unless Iraq was threatening to attack a country or demonstrably responsible for a major terrorist assault like 9/11. But what does that show? Certainly not that creating an unsustainable U.S. military presence on Iraq's borders made sense as a way to get the inspectors back into the country. If the troops had left, rather than invaded, before the summer of 2003, no doubt the weapons inspectors would have been thrown out again. What it shows is that there was no way to force long-term Iraqi compliance with weapons inspections unless Iraq was widely perceived as an ongoing and imminent threat to other nations. This is true, but scarcely a failure of containment.

Containment has never been about preventing potential adversaries from arming themselves. If that miracle could be accomplished, we would not need any national security strategy at all. Containment is about managing potential threats in a world of scarce military resources. It involves war as a last resort in response to an imminent threat. The Bush administration was unable to convince many traditional allies who had been part of the 1991 Gulf War coalition and supported the Afghanistan operation, or the UN Security Council, or even any of Iraq's neighbors— including NATO member Turkey—that it posed enough of a threat to warrant an invasion. At the very least this should have led them to wonder whether there might be disagreement within other intelligence services over Iraqi WMD comparable to those they were papering over at home. If there was consensus that Iraq was such a danger, why was there so much resistance to the proposed American action?

Sensible as it is to slow the proliferation of WMD as much as possible, it seems inevitable that diffusion of relevant know-how and technology will occur over time. Israel, North Korea, India, and Pakistan have all joined the nuclear club. Iran might well be next—followed by others. No plausible national security strategy can discount these possibilities. Once countries have nuclear arsenals, the only real options are to work with them when this is feasible, and to contain them when it is not. But a vital consideration is that the more belligerent our behavior in the world, the greater the number of hostile regimes we will need to contain, and the more costly containment is going to be.

The strident assertion of American might alienates people unnecessarily, providing ideological ammunition to those who seek to mobilize anti-American sentiment. Those who fear the United States are drawn to anti-American alliances in search of their own security, and the costs, for potential allies, of associating with us increase. Whatever the dangers of WMD proliferation, we should avoid making them worse.

All that said, the notion that the proliferation of destructive technologies by itself presents new threats from terrorists is easily exaggerated. The catastrophe that is usually conjured up here is of a nuclear suitcase bomb or a vial of a deadly biological or chemical toxin in the hands of a terrorist group—just what President Bush described in his 2003 State of the Union. Building and maintaining a viable nuclear weapon is enormously difficult. It is highly unlikely, as Thomas Schelling has recently reminded us, that a terrorist group could assemble the technological know-how and resources to pull it off.[27] This is more the stuff of James Bond movies than it is a plausible threat. To the extent that proliferation is a concern as a by-product of the collapse of the USSR, the answer has nothing to do with a "war on terror." It involves working with the Russians to secure and account for fissile materials, hiring or tracking unemployed scientists with the relevant know-how, and investing in human intelligence to learn as much as possible about groups intent on procuring them.

Much the same is true of harmful biological agents. They are hard to store, to transform into viable weapons, and actually to use. The Aum Shinrikyo religious cult that killed twelve people with sarin nerve gas in the Tokyo subway in 1995 had tried at least nine biological attacks in the preceding years—all of which failed.[28] Chemical weapons are easier to manufacture and deploy, but the threat they present is scarcely new. Indeed, much of the technology is World War I vintage.[29] Sarin itself was first developed as a pesticide in 1938.[30] None of this is to suggest that we should be unconcerned about WMD getting into the hands of terrorists, only that there is nothing in the nature of the materials themselves that presents a qualitatively new threat—and that in any case the traditional responses are the only available ones.

Intelligence and Rogue Regimes

What of the limits of intelligence that were so clearly demonstrated in Iraq? Everyone was surprised, the argument goes, by the decrepit condition of Iraq's WMD unmasked after the 2003 invasion. If Saddam had really been developing chemical and biological weapons again and was rekindling his nuclear program, as many in the intelligence communities of the West believed, would it not have been imperative to act before the threat became imminent? The alternative was seldom clearly specified, though some administration officials conjured up the image of mushroom clouds above American cities or comparably dire outcomes.[31]

The alternatives presumably are that either Iraq would itself have used such weapons against the United States or its allies, or Saddam would have supplied them to terrorists who would have done so. The first is not remotely plausible, since it would predictably have produced retaliation of annihilating proportions for Iraq. In this respect it is notable that during the 1991 Gulf War Iraq deployed no chemical or biological agents against U.S. troops, and none on the Scud missiles sent to Israel. Indeed it is questionable whether they would have sent any missiles at all had the United States not put its own troops there to man the Patriot anti-Scud missiles, forestalling any Israeli response. Israel's nuclear capacity is such that it could obliterate every Iraqi city while threatening the capitals of every country in the region that might think of joining the fray. It was simply not a plausible option for Iraq; that Saddam did not try it is further evidence that those who thought him irrational were wrong. This is not to mention that any use of WMD against Israel would have to be expected to kill or maim as many Palestinians as Israelis.

The same logic applies to Iran today. The specter of nuclear proliferation is always troubling, and there is no reason to believe Iranian claims that its uranium enrichment program is restricted to peaceful purposes. Indeed, there is evidence that the Iranians have frequently engaged in "delay, prevarication, and dissimulation" in negotiations over their nuclear agenda.[32] But such tactics scarcely distinguish them from the Soviets, against whom containment was successfully practiced. In any case, Iran is no better positioned than was Iraq to deploy nuclear weapons for anything other than defensive purposes. Even in that case it would have to be a tactic of absolute last resort, since provoking a nuclear response from Israel or the United States would for all practical purposes leave them without a country. It is not surprising, therefore, that several commentators have argued that containing a nuclear-armed Iran is a less frightening prospect than an invasion orchestrated by the Bush administration,[33] or that the new Iraqi government is unperturbed by the Iranian nuclear program.[34] As Robert

Pape points out, none of Iran's leaders since 1979 has ever shown a "reckless disregard for America's capacity to retaliate for unprovoked aggression against it, so we have no actual basis to doubt that we could live with a nuclear Iran."[35]

On the face of it the more plausible worry is that such regimes might supply terrorists with WMD to act as their proxies. There has never been even the hint of a suggestion from any intelligence source that Iraq ever contemplated this, despite the more or less cynical administration attempts to create and reinforce the groundless public perception that Iraq was somehow implicated in 9/11.[36] Indeed, in January of 2003, two months before the invasion, President Bush was informed of the unanimous view of U.S. intelligence agencies that Saddam Hussein would not try to attack the United States through surrogates unless the United States attacked Iraq in such a way as to threaten "the imminent demise of his regime." The only dissent came from the State Department's Bureau of Intelligence Research (INR), which concluded that Saddam was unlikely to sponsor clandestine attacks on the United States even if his "regime's demise is imminent."[37]

An obvious reason for the reluctance to sponsor terrorist attacks is the low probability of remaining undiscovered—subjecting the sponsoring regime to the same devastating retaliation as if they had mounted the attack themselves. There is an additional concern that, once armed, terrorist groups might be difficult to control and could come back to bite. Perhaps they would carry out the attack as directed, but perhaps not. Things change unpredictably, as American policy-makers should know. U.S. support for the Mujahideen against the Soviets in Afghanistan during the 1980s helped consolidate the strongly anti-American Taliban regime that subsequently became a haven for Al Qaeda.

In the quicksand of shifting alliances in the Middle East, today's ally might well be tomorrow's enemy and vice versa. Iran's changing relations with Iraq, and even with Iraqi Shiites, over the past two decades makes this all too clear. Perhaps the next conflict involving Iran and Iraq will be Sunni-Shiite, but it might just as likely break down along Persian-Arab lines. With Iraq's integrity as a viable state now in serious doubt, the only thing that can be said with much confidence is how unpredictable these things are. This is scarcely a situation in which governments will likely start handing out WMD to groups they have limited capacity to control and whose interests might shift suddenly, radically, and unpredictably in the relatively near future.

This leaves the notion that leaders of a regime who really believed that they were facing an imminent and devastating assault would attack—either directly or through surrogates. Perhaps INR was wrong about what Saddam Hussein would have done in extremis had he possessed WMD in 2003—despite the evidence to the contrary from 1991. Perhaps Iran might do something comparable in the future, as some were suggesting in 2006.[38] But all that shows is the danger and absurdity of cornering any regime unnecessarily. We now know how lucky the world is that President Kennedy rejected the advice of his Joint Chiefs of Staff for a preventive strike against Cuba in 1962. The Soviet forces there had tactical nuclear weapons with orders to use them to repel an invasion—which would have sparked superpower nuclear exchange.[39] It is frightening to contemplate how this might have played out had

Kennedy—chastened by the disaster that followed his listening to the generals during the Bay of Pigs the previous year—not opted for the instruments of containment instead. Unfortunately this lesson was long forgotten in the face of the poorly vetted intelligence on Iraq and the confident predictions of the Ahmed Chalabis of this world to the George W. Bush administration.

Whether there is now a learning curve that will prevent a comparable debacle in Iran remains to be seen. At the time of the Iraq invasion, Iranian expatriate supporters of Reza Pahlavi, the exiled son of the former shah, were pressing hard for regime change there as well. The hope was to restore Pahlavi as a constitutional monarch. Leaving aside questions about its desirability, it was far from clear that this was feasible. Many of those claiming that the mullah regime was on its last legs had not been in Iran for decades, raising the question whether they had any reason to believe their own claims, or—as with Chalabi in Iraq—they were being swayed by like-minded expatriates, wishful thinking, and American neoconservatives. William Kristol was pushing hard for an aggressive policy toward Iran, as was the American Israel Public Affairs Committee (AIPAC) and the Iranian Jewish Public Affairs Committee (IJPAC). Former Reagan administration officials Michael Ledeen and Frank Gaffney, ex-CIA head James Woolsey, and others formed the Coalition for Democracy in Iran to promote the idea that the time had come for Washington to push Iran over the edge.[40]

President Bush promised in his 2004 election campaign that if reelected he would make regime change in Iran a priority.[41] The threat Iran supposedly posed was a recurring mantra in the second term, including being singled out for special attention in the 2006 *National Security Strategy*. Just what the administration thought could be achieved by ratcheting up tensions with Iran—at the same time as others in the government were acknowledging that security in southern Iraq could not be attained without Iranian cooperation—was far from clear.[42] Nor was it evident that the administration had any plausible intelligence to the effect that Iran's dispersed and fortified nuclear facilities could be destroyed by an American attack, let alone that regime change was feasible.

The lessons that should be drawn from the intelligence failure in Iraq are taken up more fully in chapter 6. For now it is worth noting that every national security policy is accompanied by the risks associated with imperfect intelligence. The Soviets and Chinese developed operational nuclear weapons faster than the Truman and Johnson administrations anticipated. *Sputnik* took the Eisenhower administration by surprise. Both the Reagan and first Bush administrations underestimated how feeble the USSR was by the 1980s, and were caught off-guard by its accelerating implosion. The relevant moral to draw here is that what we saw in Iraq was a failure of intelligence, not a failure of containment. No national security policy can be better than the intelligence on which it is based. The United States would in all likelihood have been better informed about Iraqi capabilities if human intelligence had not been so seriously cut by successive administrations after the Cold War in favor of other defense priorities. This was partly due to retrenchment once the Soviet threat had dissipated, but it was also fueled by the seductive attraction of technology: the information revolution in general and satellite technology in particular.[43] The foiled plot to blow up airliners over the north Atlantic in August of 2006 dramatized all too clearly that there is no substitute for human intelligence in combating terrorist networks.

Corruption and the Erosion of Containment

Other arguments that containment was unequal to the challenges posed by Iraq focus on the instability of the sanctions regime in general and corruption associated with the oil-for-food program in particular. Sustaining the sanctions regime would have taken robust cooperation from others to help make the UN enforcement mechanisms work. The Bush administration was right that such cooperation was in short and decreasing supply, but how much of this was its own doing? Sanctions regimes, like cartels, are inherently unstable. They need active tending in order to remain effective. The strident unilateralism of the 2002 *National Security Strategy* and the administration's aggressive contempt for the UN alienated traditional allies as well as countries without any particular stake in the Iraq conflict. Spurning multilateralism has been immensely costly for the United States, as even an ex-neoconservative like Fukuyama has come to see. The notion that traditional alliances and international institutions can be augmented by the Bush Doctrine assumes that cooperation with others can be turned on and off as it suits American whims—without any attention to their needs, aspirations, and perceptions of what is legitimate. In this respect it is curious that although Fukuyama now acknowledges the need for multilateral cooperation, he continues to heap scorn on the UN as lacking legitimacy because it provides a platform for nondemocratic countries "hypocritically" to attack the United States.[44]

But there is no reason to think that the UN should insulate the United States from criticism—hypocritical or not. Its principal purpose, after all, is to reduce the likelihood of another major war by fostering international cooperation and creating a forum—the Security Council—in which the major powers have strong incentives to work to resolve differences peacefully. The Soviets and Chinese were nondemocracies that constantly denounced the United States during the Cold War, yet no U.S. administration used this as a reason to bail out of the UN or try to reform it so as to diminish their participation. The UN did its job during the Cold War just because it introduced some constraints on the conflicting agendas of major players and made it difficult for them to avoid talking to one another. This was true partly because of the unanimity rule in the Security Council, but also because the various players had to cooperate in a range of other endeavors, from managing potential new conflicts, to peacekeeping and reconstruction efforts, to development assistance and international prosecutions.

Like the Bush administration, Fukuyama seems oblivious to the ways in which institutions such as the UN can be useful in promoting a culture of cooperation to contain dangerous regimes. As Robert Keohane has pointed out, international institutions are more costly to create than they are to maintain. Indeed, it is unlikely that the United States today commands the resources to create a regime of international institutions comparable to those that grew out of the Atlantic Charter and the UN in the wake of World War II. Hence the importance of sustaining them.[45] If anything, this is more important now than it was during the Cold War just because the sources of future threats are less predictable. When the main threat came, directly or indirectly, from the USSR, heavy reliance on NATO and traditional allies brought a larger measure of security than it does when dangerous weapons are proliferating, and threats are more difficult to predict and hence to plan for. In this world, supporting international institutions is more important, not less important.

The most consequential post-9/11 legitimacy deficit in relation to the UN was the U.S. decision to invade Iraq even though Security Council authorization for the action was not forthcoming. If the most powerful country in the world shows no interest in compliance with UN norms and precedents, why should anyone else be expected to comply with them? If ever there was a case where the United States should lead by example, this is it. Instead the Bush administration demonized and defied the institution, and then inflicted a patronizing ambassador on it whose famous contempt for it meant that, even with a Republican-controlled Senate, he could get the job only through a recess appointment.[46]

The neoconservative disdain for institutions like the UN stems from the conviction that they limit U.S. flexibility in defending its interests. But as Keohane notes, maintaining flexibility creates costs of its own. National governments need others to believe that their conduct is predictable, and that they will adhere to their commitments in the future. This makes it worth working within the constraints of international institutions and international law as much as possible—even when it is irksome.[47] Yet the Bush administration's instrumental—not to say opportunistic—approach to international law mirrors its contempt for international institutions. The widely held perception that the United States is willing to flout international law, in the name of unilateralism, as it pleases has weakened the infrastructure for international cooperation on which containment depends.[48] This will make the national security job of future administrations vastly more difficult than it would otherwise have been.

As for the oil-for-food program, it had been introduced by the UN at the behest of the Clinton administration in 1995 to ameliorate the civilian hardship caused by the sanctions imposed on Iraq after the 1991 Gulf War. The idea was to let Iraq exchange oil on the world market for medicine and food, and to meet other humanitarian needs. By the time sanctions were lifted in 2003, some $65 billion worth of Iraqi oil had been sold: $46 billion of this was meant for humanitarian needs, with the balance going for war reparations and weapons inspections.[49] As would subsequently be confirmed by the Volker Commission in October of 2005, the corruption worries were real. Much of the revenue was being skimmed off in kickbacks that were finding their way into Saddam Hussein's coffers.[50]

Yet we must be careful here to compare like with like. In any full accounting of corruption, the malfeasance uncovered in the oil-for-food program must be compared to the corruption that will attend the multibillion-dollar contracts for rebuilding Iraq handed out by the United States and the interim Iraqi governments since 2003. Inklings of the scale of this criminality were beginning to come into view by late 2005. In November Robert Stein, a convicted felon who had control of $82 million in Iraq reconstruction funds, was charged with accepting kickbacks and bribes in the distribution of contracts.[51] The following week Republican congressman Randy "Duke" Cunningham of California pled guilty to accepting $2.4 million in bribes from defense contractors. It was the largest case of congressional bribery in American history and would eventually net him an eight-year prison sentence.[52] Then there was the security firm Custer Battles, alleged to have charged the U.S. government many millions of dollars for spurious services and materials.[53] No doubt these examples will turn out to be the tips of various icebergs, with billions of dollars concededly unaccounted for by early 2006.[54] This is to say nothing of Iraqi corruption, surely in the hundreds of millions of dollars at least. Much of it doubly undermines the rebuilding effort by winding up in the pockets of insurgents.[55]

Moreover, the oil-for-food program could have been reformed to reduce the corruption. A major design flaw was that it allowed Saddam to choose which foreign firms to deal with, making the entire panoply of skimming and kickbacks that subsequently developed more or less inevitable from the outset.[56] This could have been changed, some major culprits could have been prosecuted, and better UN oversight mechanisms could have been introduced. Corruption could have been substantially reduced, perhaps below the levels we are seeing in Iraq now and will likely see in the future. The idea that weaknesses in UN enforcement merited giving up ignores reality. Corruption cannot be eliminated completely, and enforcement regimes are invariably works in progress.

The Beliefs of Attackers

A different set of reasons that lead some to question containment's adequacy to the task of combating terrorism concerns the messianic motives of attackers. Sometimes this concern is directed at the attackers themselves (usually sui- cide bombers), sometimes at the leaders of terrorist groups, and sometimes at the leaders of enabling regimes. Noting that Kennan himself doubted whether containment would have worked against figures like Napoleon, who lacked "the caution that Marxism-Leninism had instilled in Soviet lead- ers," John Gaddis suggests that terrorists and their enablers might be insufficiently calculating—or perhaps not calcu- lating in the right ways—to be influenced by its logic.[57] But it is far from clear that the leaders of Iran and North Korea are more like Napoleon than like Stalin on this dimension. Saddam Hussein was famous for being highly calculating in his dealings with the West. Indeed, there is reason to think that his miscalculation in invading Kuwait in 1990 was based on mixed signals from the first Bush administration as to what the likely U.S. response would be.[58] If so, that makes it a *failure to contain*, not a *failure of containment*.

When adversaries are indeed unresponsive to any avail- able incentives, as might be true of suicide bombers and some political leaders, this means that they cannot be de- terred from attempting aggression. But it does not mean that they cannot be contained. Bullies, wife-batterers, and psychotics are sometimes not deterrable—but they are containable. Just how far one has to go in order to keep them contained varies with the perpetrator, the circum- stances, and the available tools. In Saddam Hussein's case af- ter the 1991 Gulf War, the judgment was that he had liter- ally to be hemmed into the middle third of his country.[59] Far from suggesting that rogue states defy the logic of con- tainment, Saddam Hussein's Iraq illustrates how contain- ment can work. A similar story could be told about North Korea. There, ironically in view of the Bush administration's rejection of containment in Iraq, they have revived what for all practical purposes was the Clinton administration's policy of containment—insisting on multilateral negotiations in concert with regional powers as a condition for doing business with the regime. However, as Nicholas Kristof has noted, the Bush administration's aggressive demonization of the regime since the "Axis of Evil" speech has made the task much more difficult. The North Korean plutonium enrichment program, which had been shelved during the regime's agreement with the Clinton administration, was restarted in response to the Bush policy.[60]

Perhaps the more plausible version of the objection concerns the beliefs of terrorist leaders and the suicide bombers they send. The scary images here are of gullible youth in refugee camps, deranged individuals, messianic religious fanatics, and others easily programmed for deadly missions of maximum destruction. People who are willing to die, even want to die, in the course of their attacks seem manifestly beyond the reach of incentives and the traditional instruments of containment. Punishments, at least the punishments that can be meted out in this world, will not stop people, as President Bush puts it, "whose only goal is death." On this understanding, the problem is the messianic beliefs themselves.[61]

In reality there is no particular connection between Islam, fundamentalism, or even religious belief, and willingness to die in suicide missions. Suicide attackers have been around for millennia. Over the past century they have ranged from Japanese kamikaze pilots to adherents of many religions, to nationalists of various sorts, to the decidedly secular Marxist group the Tamil Tigers of Sri Lanka. Suicide attackers come from many milieus, religious and secular, and various socioeconomic groups. Several of the 9/11 attackers were famously both middle-aged and middle-class. Suicide killers are, therefore, neither new nor intrinsically linked to Islam. In fact the Tamil Tigers have engaged in more suicide attacks than any other group in recent decades.[62] Even in a self-consciously Islamist group like Hezbollah, Robert Pape found that of the forty-one attackers involved in suicide missions between 1982 and 1986, only eight were affiliated with Islamic fundamentalism.[63]

Focusing on the bombers themselves, while riveting, in any case misses the doughnut for the hole. Learning more about what was in the heads of the kamikaze pilots would tell us nothing about why they were sent—and they would scarcely have gone on their own. It is highly unusual for a terrorist attack to be the act of a lone individual or a small self-motivated group. The 1995 Oklahoma City bombing is the most dramatic case in recent times. But the "war on terror" was not prompted by such rare events, which will inevitably be handled through the criminal justice system—even in the post-9/11 era. For the most part, suicide attackers and perpetrators of other forms of extreme terrorism do not act alone. Individual bombers need organizations, and organizations are not immune from containment and disruption strategies. The relevant focus for a national security policy is those who plan and orchestrate the missions. They play by different rules from those of the bombers they deploy.

The Beliefs of Terrorist Leaders

Are those who plan and direct terrorist missions sufficiently messianic in their beliefs or irrational in their agendas that they defy the traditional tools of containment? The suggestion that the leaders of the major Islamist terrorist groups are beyond strategic calculation and response, or that they seek either perpetual conflict or world domination, reveals, more than anything else, ignorance about their goals. Both the PLO and Hamas have restricted their targets to Israelis, and Hamas has never attacked anyone outside the Middle East. Hezbollah has attacked Americans only in Lebanon. Iraqi insurgents never attacked anyone outside of Iraq until more than two and a half years after the American invasion. Even Al Qaeda sees itself as engaged in a defensive jihad, as I have noted, not a bid to take over the world or wipe out the American way of life. Nor is it clear that bin Laden's behavior is beyond the logic of incentives. By some accounts, he was bribed by the Saudi regime after 1991 to keep his activities out of Saudi Arabia.[64] The leaders of all these groups see themselves as engaged in struggles of national or regional liberation, trying to overthrow corrupt regimes, expelling an imperial military presence from their part of the world, or some combination of these.[65] This is not to say that all their aspirations can or should be accommodated. It is to say, however, that we cannot respond sensibly to the threat that they pose without understanding what motivates them and gives them the resources to pose the threats that they do.

Ill-informed pronouncements on the irrationality of these groups abound among Western commentators and governments. For instance, five years after Yitzhak Rabin's assassination Ehud Barak and Bill Clinton dusted off what was essentially the same deal that Yasser Arafat had been willing to sign up to in 1995, and put it back on the table at Camp David. This time he rejected it—prompting many to repeat Abba Eban's old line that Arafat "never misses an opportunity to miss an opportunity."[66] Far from reflecting Arafat's irrationality, though, his intransigence was a reasonable response to changes in Palestinian politics and his place in them that had occurred in the intervening five years. His visibly corrupt Palestinian Authority had lost legitimacy. Years of humiliation at the hands of successive Israeli governments, plus the failure to deliver material improvements, had eroded his personal prestige among Palestinians. The growth and popularity of other groups, particularly Hamas, had accelerated, with the result that Arafat would probably not have lasted a week in Palestinian politics had he signed on at Camp David in 2000.[67] The problem was not that Palestinian leaders are irrational. Arafat played his hand the only way he could. Clinton and Barak failed to realize that he was by then too weak to deliver a settlement, and that other Palestinian leaders must now be dealt with.

This disconnect has persisted into the post–Arafat era. In January of 2005 Hamas comfortably won the local elections in Gaza, prompting his successor, Mahmoud Abbas, to postpone general Palestinian Authority elections scheduled for July for fear of losing them. The following December Hamas easily won the local elections in the West Bank, and a month later was swept into power on a landslide in the delayed elections for the Palestinian parliament. Secretary of State Condoleezza Rice responded by demanding an investigation into why the U.S. administration had been surprised by the outcome.[68] The real question was how anyone who had been paying attention to Palestinian politics over the preceding several years could possibly have been surprised.[69] That Secretary Rice would make such a comment was a chilling illustration of the degree to which the Bush administration gets information from its own echo chamber; it is reminiscent of Vice President Cheney's repeated insistence that the Iraqi insurgency was in its "last throes" while the number of insurgents there steadily grew.[70] Secretary Rice's comment also reflects the common American propensity to confuse leaders the United States might regard as desirable with leaders who actually enjoy legitimacy on the ground. As Yitzhak Rabin noted in 1993, people do not need to negotiate peace agreements with their friends.[71]

But the more significant reality the Bush administration was missing was that the Hamas leadership had for some time been signaling interest in an end to violence and a settlement with Israel. This began with a unilateral cease-fire agreed with the Palestinian Authority in June of 2003. This fell apart when a West Jerusalem bus bombing by a rogue Hamas cell from Hebron (disowned by the Hamas leadership) produced massive Israeli retaliation, including the assassination of Ismail Abu Shanab—the main Hamas architect of the cease-fire—among others. The bus bombing was a catalyst for concerted multilateral containment of Hamas. The European Union put the whole organization (not just its military wing) on their terrorism blacklist, funds of sister organizations were sequestered in Israel and elsewhere, and economic support from Arab states declined sharply.[72]

At the same time, Hamas was becoming an increasingly successful political force in Gaza and the West Bank. Yasser Arafat's corrupt and ineffective Palestinian Authority had lost popularity in the last years of his life. Hamas was operating as the de facto welfare state—especially in Gaza.

Israel's killing many of its military leaders after 2003 and jailing charismatic figures like Raed Salah boosted their popularity. Nowhere was Hamas's increased political confidence and strength more clearly underscored than in the Cairo Accord with Arafat's successor Mahmoud Abbas in March of 2005. Hamas agreed to a lull in terrorist operations *in exchange for* the new elections to the PA, which would bring them to power the following year.[73] This was a dramatic shift from their boycott of the 1996 elections. Quite possibly it reflected their discovery of what groups like the Euskadi ta Askatasuna (ETA) Basque separatists had learned before them: that popular support tends to be eroded by extreme forms of terrorism.[74] Certainly Hamas's move was widely welcomed: 73 percent of Palestinians supported its decision to participate in elections, and more than 61 percent thought that if Hamas became part of the Palestinian Legislative Council, it would abide by council decisions.[75]

The combination of military defeats and political strength led Hamas to adopt a new truce in January of 2005, indicating that it would be made permanent if Abbas—now PA president following Arafat's death—could get assurances of Israeli reciprocity and released Palestinian prisoners. Sharon rejected the offer, noting only that "quiet will be met with quiet."[76] Hamas continued the truce nonetheless and, following its 2006 election victory, began floating trial balloons suggesting willingness to recognize Israel as an "occupier state"; the possibility of establishing a Palestinian state within "provisional borders," as outlined in the U.S. road map, as an interim solution on the way to a two-state solution based on the 1967 boundaries; and a long-term (perhaps ten-year) *hudna* or truce.[77] The Hamas leadership was also quick publicly to reject Al Qaeda's offer of support and its advice never to make peace with Israel in the wake of its international isolation and ostracism after its 2006 election victory.[78]

The continued refusal to consider disarming or to accept Israel's legitimacy led their offers to fall on deaf ears in Jerusalem and Washington—where these remained preconditions for negotiations. Insisting on such preconditions is misguided. As the International Crisis Group's 2004 report on "Dealing with Hamas" noted, waiting for the emergence of a "reliable Palestinian partner" is bound to be "a recipe for paralysis, or worse: only a credible political process can produce an effective Palestinian leadership, not the other way around."[79]

A South African comparison might be instructive here. When the apartheid government decided in 1990 to unban the ANC and all other political groups, release all political prisoners, and begin negotiations, the ANC had neither recognized the government's legitimacy nor suspended its armed struggle. Most white South Africans feared the ANC as an agent of the USSR—not least because its leadership overlapped with that of one of the most Stalinist communist parties in the world. During the on-again-off-again negotiations over the next two years, the ANC refused requests to decommission weapons or accept that the government's insistence on constitutionally mandated "power sharing" would ever be part of a settlement. At the time, power sharing was considered by most whites nonnegotiable. Nonetheless, the government continued negotiating with the ANC even after multiparty talks twice broke down—leading eventually to a settlement and democratic elections in 1994.[80]

As President DeKlerk subsequently explained to me, what gave both him and Mandela room to maneuver was the fact that neither made negotiating dependent on the other side's acceptance of conditions or benchmark achievements. That would have provided targets for spoilers on both sides who were determined to kill the possibility of an agreement.[81] Their absence made it possible for the reformers in the government and the moderates in the ANC to produce results, moving the process forward and enhancing their legitimacy. The repeated failure of lulls, truces, and agreements in the Palestinian-Israeli conflict for just this reason has been seen many times.[82]

Whether a settlement with Hamas could in fact be negotiated is an open question, but it is far from clear that it could not. There is little in Hamas's actions over the past several years to suggest that its leadership is unresponsive to the logic of containment or incapable of strategic compromise. But Israel and the U.S. administration have first to come to grips with the reality that Hamas's legitimacy on the ground means that they must be dealt with. Rather than demonize Hamas and try to engineer its collapse, it would be better, as one analyst of Palestinian affairs has said, to deploy "incentives and pressures designed to strengthen the more pragmatic and accommodationist within Hamas who aspire to join the Palestinian national consensus."[83] This would involve active engagement with the more pragmatic "internal" Hamas leadership led most prominently by Ismail Haniyeh and Mahmoud al-Zahar, as distinct from the more ideological "outside" leaders—Khaled Masha'al and Musa Abu Marzuk.[84]

The likely costs of not pressing forward, taking advantage of the gains that were on offer during the sixteen-month truce, were poignantly underscored in early June of 2006. An apparently errant Israeli rocket killed eight civilians on a Gaza beach, leading Hamas leaders to suspend the truce—promising reprisal attacks on Israeli civilians.[85] Cognizant of Al Qaeda's presence in Gaza, which had been growing as they moved toward being a government that might negotiate a settlement, Hamas leaders were protecting their flank.[86] Lacking any prospect of a tangible result, Hamas risked losing the symbols of Palestinian liberation to Al Qaeda just as the PLO had lost them to Hamas when Yitzhak Rabin's assassination scuttled the agreement he had been close to reaching with Arafat in 1995.[87] The window of opportunity seemed again to be closing.

Some might concede that organizations like Hamas have strategic goals that make them open to the logic of incentives, yet insist that this sets them apart from transnational Islamist groups with their global ambitions and choice of targets. Olivier Roy suggests that this is increasingly so with Al Qaeda. Since the 1990s, fueled partly by its success against the Soviets in Afghanistan, partly by the recruitment of new cadres of operatives in Europe, and partly as a response to the global expansion of U.S. power, at least some in Al Qaeda have been less interested in a defensive jihad and more attracted to "an imaginary *ummah* (community) that is everywhere and nowhere." On Roy's account Al Qaeda now "has no strategic vision. It fights against Babylon, against what it sees as evil, the United States and its ally, Israel." Many of its targets, he notes, have no military or strategic value—nightclubs and restaurants in Bali and Casablanca or a synagogue on the Tunisian island of Jerba.[88]

Roy's reasoning can be questioned on the grounds that, however imaginary its goals, Al Qaeda must still make strategic decisions—rendering its leaders subject to logics of incentives. The disagreement in July of 2005, aired in a letter from bin Laden's chief lieutenant Ayman Zawahiri to Iraqi insurgent leader Abu Musab Zarqawi, is a case in point. Attempting to rein Zarqawi in, Zawahiri criticized beheadings and other extreme measures as undermining the indigenous support that would be needed for Al Qaeda after the inevitable American departure from Iraq.[89] But even conceding Roy's point, up to a point, what follows? It is far from clear that endless "war on terror" (not notably less inchoate than the idea of a global ummah) will reduce the supply of this sort of terrorist. On the contrary, the evidence from Iraq is that it increases that supply. The sensible approach is, rather, to avoid stimulating the supply and to limit Al Qaeda's access to resources and support. As Roy notes, the weaknesses of Al Qaeda are its perpetual need of sanctuaries and the difficulty for its militants' struggles to establish social and political bases without the support of local allies.[90] The logic of containment suggests taking advantage of these weaknesses. Shift the focus away from the content of their beliefs to the conditions that make it less likely that they will find sanctuary and indigenous support.

An additional factor to focus on here is money. Particularly for transnational terrorist groups that lack permanent sanctuaries and must operate at great distances from their targets, tracing the movement of money can be a helpful tool of intelligence and containment. It is fashionable to note that the actual cost of a given terrorist attack is quite small, suggesting that efforts at financial counterterrorism are a bit like trying to stop a needle with a haystack. But this is akin to saying that the cost to a restaurant of producing a single meal is small; it ignores the costs of building, maintaining, and operating the restaurant. Even Al Qaeda, with its unusual access to bin Laden's personal fortune, must perpetually raise millions of dollars to fund its infrastructure, training camps, and other activities, and move that money around the world.[91]

Some of this is done through *hawala*—informal credit and banking services that operate out of mosques and small businesses with a minimum of paperwork and no reliance on banks. This might suggest that there is limited utility to heeding the advice of William Wechsler, former director for national threats of the NSC in the Clinton administration, that we "follow the money."[92] But what it really signals is one more reason to invest in human intelligence. Tracing the fund-raising and hawala transfers is a retail activity, not a wholesale one. It depends on cooperation with regional allies and infiltration of terrorist cells, mosques, and hawala networks.

But the banking system is by no means irrelevant. Terrorist groups whose leaders must direct operations in Western countries from afar will likely have to use banks—as, indeed, the 9/11 hijackers did. They accessed funds through ATMs. A common observation on the attacks was that the ease with which funds can now be transferred around the world in this way works to their advantage. But the flip side of this truth is that these funds are easily traceable. Tracking financial transfers was vital, for instance, in breaking open the conspiracy to blow up airliners over the north Atlantic in August of 2006.[93] This gives banks and governments incentives to cooperate in reporting suspicious movements of funds. But that requires multilateral cooperation with the relevant governments and financial institutions.[94]

Transnational Terror Networks and Weak States

Critics of containment in the face of terrorism contend that the transnational character of modern terrorist organizations renders obsolete a doctrine that was designed for conventional, if aggressive, nation-states. "Shadowy terrorist networks," as President Bush says, "are not easily contained." As John Gaddis puts it, containment was conceived as a state-based strategy focused on "identifiable regimes that could manage the running of risks short of war."[95] As a result, containment seems to lack purchase on international terrorist groups. They are not part of the chess game of international diplomacy and not susceptible, therefore, to the incentives and cost-benefit calculations that govern it.

But this conclusion underestimates the extent to which terrorist groups rely, to do their business, on enabling states. As Senator John McCain put it on the Don Imus radio show, the threats terrorist organizations pose are greatly magnified when they are sponsored by states because their "training, equipment, and capabilities are dramatically increased."[96] How much weaker would the PLO have been without territorial bases in Egypt, Jordan, Syria, Lebanon, and elsewhere between the 1960s and 1980s?[97] Bin Laden and Al Qaeda were vitally dependent on the Taliban regime in Afghanistan in the run-up to 9/11. Saudi Arabia had expelled them for antigovernment activities in 1991 and successfully pressured Sudan to drive them out of Khartoum three years later. Afghanistan, where they had fought the Soviets during the 1980s, was their only sanctuary.

Terrorist groups might not themselves always be feasible targets of containment, but enabling regimes certainly can be. Libya has, after all, been induced to change its behavior by the persistent application of sanctions and other classic tools of containment. The Taliban regime could have survived in Afghanistan had it turned over bin Laden and closed the Al Qaeda bases, as demanded by the United States immediately following 9/11. Mullah Omar's refusal to do so forced the subsequent escalation. The diversion of U.S. attention and resources—previously applied to rooting out the sanctuaries in Afghanistan and Pakistan and now funding the Iraq adventure—has contributed to whatever continuing threat Al Qaeda poses. It is difficult to imagine a terrorist group without territorial sanctuary presenting a serious, ongoing threat to U.S. national security. It was, after all, rogue *states* that were identified by President Bush as constituting the "Axis of Evil." There is no intrinsic reason to suppose them less containable than the "Evil Empire" identified by President Reagan.

Indeed, as Pauline Jones Luong and Ellen Lust-Okar have noted, Islamists who either come to power in national states or approach the possibility of it will increasingly find themselves at odds with transnational Islamist groups like Al Qaeda. The business of consolidating and operating a regime is bound to involve imperatives and compromises that the transnational group has no reason to support and will likely reject—most obviously building broad coalitions of national support.[98] We saw this with Hamas's rejection of Al Qaeda's post-2006 election advice not to embrace a two-state solution that would implicitly concede Israel's sovereignty. We saw it with Iran's cooperation with the Northern Alliance and the United States in

Afghanistan after 9/11. The Iranian regime was no friend of Al Qaeda and was happy to see their Taliban enablers wiped away. And we saw the limiting case of the tension in Afghanistan itself. Mullah Omar's inability to reconcile the demands of being a functioning state in the international order with continuing to provide a haven for Al Qaeda cost his Taliban regime its existence.

The most fruitful way to think about the tension between national and transnational Islamist groups is to press it into the service of containment. To the extent that nationalist movements and governments support international terrorist groups, we should retaliate with the traditional tools: diplomatic pressure, sanctions, international law enforcement, and whatever other incentives can be brought to bear. But there are two reasons to welcome the tensions that develop between national Islamist movements and governments, on the one hand, and international Islamist terrorist groups like Al Qaeda, on the other. One reason is that consolidation of national power often by itself has a moderating effect on the propensity to export terrorism. As we have seen with the by and large successful integration of Islamist groups in Turkey and Jordan, fledgling governments must solve a host of domestic problems that do not concern terrorist organizations. They also need international cooperation to have any hope of building viable economies and modern infrastructures. Accordingly, they are more likely to behave as the PLO did in the mid-1990s and Hamas did during its sixteen-month 2005–6 truce.[99] (The flip side of this logic is that if Hamas's chances of becoming a fledgling government fade, their conflicts of interest with Al Qaeda will diminish as well.)

We should also welcome tensions between national and

international Islamist movements for the reasons Kennan welcomed tensions between the Soviets and others in the international communist movement. As agendas diverge, the resulting competition confronts the United States with a less monolithic adversary. It also diffuses the costs of combating international Islamist terror groups like Al Qaeda. Until 2003, Saudi Arabia largely went through the motions of assisting with financial counterterrorism measures against Al Qaeda, fueled, perhaps, by a tacit understanding with bin Laden that he would keep his activities elsewhere. But that changed dramatically in May of that year, when Al Qaeda began a series of bombings of foreign housing compounds and other targets in Riyadh, Yanbu, and Khobar. This prompted sustained Saudi crackdowns to disrupt domestic Al Qaeda cells, improve law enforcement, and cooperate with intelligence on Al Qaeda fundraising and money laundering.[100] This was noteworthy, since Saudi Arabia had been what David Aufhauser, general counsel of the Treasury and chair of the NSC's Policy Coordinating Committee on Terrorist Financing, had described as the "epicenter" of terrorist financing.[101]

This is not to say that we should prop up the Saudi regime or underwrite its domestic repression. We should use the instruments at our disposal to pressure the Saudis in the direction of democratic reform. But, by the same token, we should not be looking to bump off the Saudi regime. Aspiring to do that exceeds our capacity for legitimate international action, not to mention American resources. We should be working to help the spread of democracy around the world as I describe in chapter 6, but this does not extend to gratuitous regime change in countries that pose no threat to the United States.

A different objection to containment advanced by defenders of the Bush Doctrine is not that terrorist havens are too strong to be deterred, but rather that they are too weak. Containment is a state-based strategy premised on the idea that governments have control of what goes on within their borders. Even if the Taliban government in Afghanistan had wanted to close down the Al Qaeda bases and turn over bin Laden as was demanded after 9/11, perhaps they would not have been able to do this. After all, the cooperating Musharraf regime in Pakistan has been unable to deliver bin Laden in the more than four years since he eluded American forces at Tora Bora and slipped over the White Mountains.

The national security challenges posed by weak states are indeed serious. Recognizing this is, however, a giant non sequitur as a defense of the Bush Doctrine, which offers no viable strategy for dealing with them. On the contrary, it seems most likely to lead to their proliferation. There are many more weak states than the United States could possibly invade and transform into functioning ones. Notably, the United States has not managed to do this in Afghanistan, where the writ of the Karzai government does not run much outside Kabul four and a half years after the Taliban was toppled. As for Iraq, whatever else it was before the U.S.-led invasion, it was a functioning state. Within the constraints imposed by the no-fly zones, Saddam Hussein's regime monopolized the instruments of public coercion at least as much as most conventional governments do. That cannot be said of postinvasion Iraq, with the ironic consequence that however many weak states there were in the world before the Iraq invasion, there is at least one more after it. And it is a weak state that could disintegrate into three weak states in the event that civil war ends up dismembering the country.

There is no realistic alternative to containment when it comes to weak states that shelter terrorist networks. In the medium term the termination of civil wars that plague many of them, help with the growth of institutional infrastructure, and development assistance that sparks sustainable economic growth might turn more of them into viable national states. But in the short term the three most important aids to contain the threats emanating from them will involve securing their borders, getting good intelligence about the groups operating within them, and working with whatever international agencies are seeking to resolve their internal conflicts and development problems. These agencies, and particularly their local representatives, are likely to be the best sources of reliable intelligence and of viable strategies to curtail the activities of terrorist groups.

Containment of weak states is especially dependent on multilateral cooperation in the local region. All the saber rattling between the United States and Iran notwithstanding, it is inconceivable that southeastern Iraq can be stabilized without Iranian cooperation—as at least some in the Bush administration have begun to acknowledge.[102] Nor is the northwestern part of the country likely to be secured without Syrian help. In 2006 Iraq's borders remained porous to terrorist traffic in both directions. Achieving the regional cooperation needed to stabilize weak states always requires cooperation with local neighbors who have the most at stake, the most relevant information, and often the capacity to be spoilers if they choose. Threatening the gov-

ernments in the neighborhood unnecessarily and advertising
hopes for domino effects of regime toppling is scarcely the
way to achieve that cooperation.

Defeating Terrorists and Manufacturing More

Containment should also be judged a realistic basis for national security in the post-9/11 era when we consider the
costs of flouting it as the advocates of the Bush Doctrine
have done. Just because an invading United States will inevitably be cast in the role of the hypocritical imperialist,
the Bush Doctrine plays into the hands of its adversaries. It
creates fodder for anti-Americanism—fueled by ethnic,
religious, and nationalist antipathies that the Bush Doctrine is bound to intensify. Terrorists and leaders of rogue
regimes can easily use the facts of U.S. behavior to rally
supporters to their causes. The inevitable abuses that occur
in wartime—the My Lais, Guantánamos, Abu Ghraibs, and
Hadithas—give them additional propaganda victories and
force the United States onto the defensive. The public
opinion data on changed perceptions of the United States
since the Iraq invasion is dramatic. Peter Katzenstein and
Robert Keohane report that polls in most countries
showed a predominantly favorable opinion of the United
States before the invasion, but this changed in 2003 and
2004—with particularly strong negative opinion register-
ing in the Middle East, North Africa, and Pakistan.[103]

This is not to mention the commonplace observation
that the U.S. invasion has been a gift to Al Qaeda—
enhancing its recruitment and turning Iraq into a magnet
for foreign fighters. Their numbers are estimated to have

grown from 100 in May of 2003 to 500 in May of 2004, to 1,000 in May of 2005, and 1,500 in May of 2006.[104] Difficult as it often is to mobilize the victims of authoritarian oppression to take the huge risks associated with opposing their oppressors, it makes little sense to offer up an alternative object of ire toward which dissatisfaction can be mobilized. That is exactly what the United States has done by invading Iraq. The conundrum we now face there calls to mind the cartoon of a Likud politician declaring that "our policy toward the Palestinians is simple: we will keep beating them until they stop hating us." Martyred terrorists have brothers, sisters, sons, and daughters—some of whom will join the cause in the fallen terrorist's place. Containment avoids these pitfalls just because it involves resisting the impulse toward domination that in turn sparks resistance.

President Bush and other defenders of the Iraq war have made the contrary case, claiming that the demonstration effect of the Iraq war has been to render rogue regimes more cooperative—for fear that they will be next. Congressman Tom Lantos, for example, has spoken of the "pedagogic value" of the war in persuading Libya to abandon its nuclear program and cooperate in the war against terror.[105] But Qaddafi had been knocking on the door for years, pulled by the allure of shedding sanctions and reintegrating with the world economy.[106] In 1996 the State Department's report on global terrorism noted a sharp reduction in Libyan sponsorship of terrorism owing to UN sanctions.[107] Three years later the Libyans extradited two Pan Am 103 bombers for trial in the Hague.[108] They also agreed to pay the French government $31 million in victims' compensation for the bombing of flight UTA 772 a decade earlier,[109] and to compensate the family of British policewoman Yvonne Fletcher, who had been shot at a demonstration outside the Libyan embassy in London.[110]

Flynt Leverett, director for Middle Eastern affairs at the NSC from 2002 to 2003, writes that the Iraq war, which had not started, "was not the driving force behind Libya's move" to abandon its nuclear program. Instead, Qaddafi was responding to an explicit quid pro quo. "American officials indicated that a verifiable dismantling of Libya's weapons projects would lead to the removal of our own sanctions."[111] Both the Clinton and George H. W. Bush administrations had brushed off similar Libyan overtures because the Libyan weapons program was not seen as an imminent threat. Qadaffi immediately condemned the 9/11 attacks, calling the Taliban "Godless promoters of political Islam."[112] In 2002, Libya signed the 1999 Convention for the Suppression of the Financing of Terrorism and the 1991 Convention on the Marking of Plastic Explosives for the Purpose of Detection.[113] The Iraq invasion was not needed to rein in Qadaffi. Indeed, instead of Iraq's serving as a model for Libya, Libya should have served as the model for U.S. policy in Iraq—as it should be guiding us in Iran.

Another positive demonstration effect sometimes claimed for the Iraq invasion has been in Lebanon. In March of 2005 Jonathan Freedland credited the "benign chain reaction" of Iraqi regime change for the mass demonstrations following the assassination of former Lebanese prime minister Rafik Hariri the previous month in which the Syrians were widely believed to have been implicated.[114] Prescient as Freedland turned out to be that the demonstrations in Beirut, buttressed by U.S. pressure, would "send the Syrians packing," it is hard, as former U.S. ambassador to Israel Martin Indyk has noted, to make a case that this was a result of the Iraq invasion.[115] It is, moreover, a tragic mis-reading of the effect of the Iraq war on Syria's involvement in Lebanon to suppose it to have boosted the prospects for democracy there.

By 2005 a Washington consensus had emerged that Syria was a destructive force that should be expelled from Lebanon. However, this was a reversal of almost three decades of cooperation dating back to Henry Kissinger's agreement to their coming in to stabilize the country in 1976.[116] Kissinger's decision embodied a widespread belief in Washington, which would persist through successive Republican and Democratic administrations until 2001, that only the Syrians could hold Lebanon together—at least in the short run.[117] That belief was reaffirmed in the run-up to the 1991 Gulf War, in which Syria supported the U.S.-led coalition against Iraq. Secretary of State James Baker III gave Damascus a green light to gain unhindered control over Lebanon, which it did.[118]

The Syrians stopped cooperating with the U.S.-led military policies in the region during the run-up to the 2003 war in Iraq. Having failed in their support of Saddam Hussein against the U.S.-led invasion, the Syrians then turned their support to the insurgency. Their about-face via-à-vis the United States seems to have been born of the belief that, unless the United States failed or became bogged down in Iraq, Syria would be next.[119] This was a reasonable fear. The Assad government in Damascus was the only other Ba'thist regime besides Saddam Hussein's Iraq, and there was open speculation in U.S. government and neoconservative circles at the time that Syria might indeed be next.

As things played out, the Syrians' departure compounded the failed-state problem in Lebanon. In September of 2004, UN Security Council Resolution 1559 had called for Syrian troops to leave Lebanon *and* for all militias to be disbanded.[120] Because only the first of these things happened, Hezbollah's power predictably expanded to fill the vacuum created by the Syrian departure.[121] There had been some expectation that the Lebanese army would be strengthened so as to enable it to control Hezbollah, but little thought seems to have been given to how this would be achieved. It would have been difficult, not least because some 40 percent of its soldiers are, like Hezbollah, Shiites. As one observer noted, "it would be a bit like the U.S. Army moving against the South."[122]

Elections were held in May and June of 2005. The anti-Syrian Tayyar-al-Mustaqbal opposition coalition led by Said Hariri, the thirty-five-year-old son of the assassinated former prime minister, became the dominant bloc with 72 seats in the parliament. However, Hezbollah won 14 seats and, with its allied Amal Party led by former military officer and one of Syria's main collaborators in Lebanon Nabih Berri, became the next largest group. With 35 seats—only one fewer than the largest party in the governing coalition—this "Resistance and Development Bloc" controlled 27 percent of the legislature. But they also had two cabinet ministers, allies in the blocs controlled by the Shiite Speaker of the House, Nabih Berri, and support from the Christian general and former prime minister Michel Aoun. As a result, they were able to use their political strength to frustrate attempts to strengthen the Lebanese army.[123]

Disarming insurgents and militias should never be a

precondition for negotiations, as I have argued, but elections are another matter. Keen to produce tangible evidence that democracy was indeed spreading through the region, the Bush administration pushed hard for the elections to proceed. Apparently they were oblivious of the reality that democracy is good for many things, but rescuing failed states and ending civil wars are not among them. Politics is not always war by other means, but it is likely to be that when the institutions of public coercion are as intensely contested as they were in Lebanon in 2005. The South African transition was greatly helped because Umkhonto we Sizwe, the military wing of the ANC, was incorporated into the army a year before the 1994 elections. Whether something analogous might have become feasible in Lebanon will never be known. But in view of the subsequent unfolding of events between Hezbollah and Israel, it would be hard to make a plausible case that the Bush administration's policy in Iraq has been advantageous for democracy's medium-run prospects in Lebanon.[124]

Whatever positive demonstration effect the Iraq war might initially have had on neighboring regimes, this was dissipated by the manifest American quagmire that developed subsequently. By early 2006 Iran had drawn the opposite moral from that intended by the administration. Why would it not? The U.S. inability to quell Iraq, coupled with the massive unpopularity of the war and the administration at home, made it obvious that no U.S. invasion of Iran was in the cards.[125] This reality drove the administration back toward the instruments of containment—working with the International Atomic Energy Agency to refer Iran to the Security Council, building multilateral support for sanctions, and cooperating with the French and Russians as back channels to come up with incentives for the Iranian leadership to back down. Containment was becoming the policy because it is the only viable option. But the task of implementing it had been made immensely more difficult owing to the damage wrought by the Bush Doctrine.

6 Democracy for Containment

The argument for containment defended here is rooted in a commitment to democracy. Its goal is to preserve existing democracies into the future by containing threats to them. Whereas George Kennan argued for containment on purely strategic grounds, my case is buttressed by the claim that containment flows naturally out of the democratic understanding of nondomination. Resisting domination by others without seeking to dominate them is the national security analogue of Machiavelli's dictum that power is best given to the common people, whose desire is not to be dominated, rather than to dominate. It bids us to work toward a world in which aggression is never met with appeasement, while at the same time avoiding the unwise temptation to try to remake the world in America's image.

Since this defense of containment appeals to the democratic ideal and is geared to preserving existing democracies into the future, it would be surprising if those who find it appealing were indifferent to the possibility of democracy's spread around the world. The commitment to nondomination means that democracy is not easily imposed at the point of a gun, as we have seen. Trying to install democracy by force should never be attempted lightly. The low odds of success are matched by the high costs of trying. These odds improve if the installation is widely seen as a legitimate international response to an aggressor regime, as with Germany and Japan in 1945, but, as the history of those cases underscores, a vast investment will certainly still be required. When the invasion lacks legitimacy, as with the 2003 U.S. invasion of Iraq, the obligation to try to foster democracy remains, while the chances of success diminish. "If you break it," Colin Powell warned President Bush on the eve of the invasion, "you own it."[1]

By late 2006 it was debatable, to say the least, whether Iraq could be stabilized, let alone stabilized as a functioning democracy. The burning question, in the run-up to the U.S. November election, was how to resolve the Hobson's choice over whether to set a date for the American departure. Opponents, such as Connecticut Senator Joseph Lieberman, counseled that this would exacerbate the incipient civil war by giving the insurgents a license simply to wait. Plausible as this was, taking this stance cost him his party's nomination in the Democratic primary.

Perhaps the reason he lost was that the primary voters recognized that the alternative is worse. Lieberman was in effect asking us to wait for the burgeoning failure in Iraq to produce success. The administration's position, which Lieberman endorsed, is that "As Iraqis stand up, we will stand down."[2] This is like telling a teenager that you will keep supporting him until he starts earning a living. Setting a date for the United States to depart is preferable, therefore, because it will force the Iraqi government to try to rise to the security challenges before we go. Otherwise there will certainly be a collapse when the costs, measured in American blood, treasure, and public opinion, force a withdrawal regardless of the situation on the ground in Iraq.

Important as it is to set a date for the U.S. departure, it is yet more important to start planning for U.S. policy toward post-occupation Iraq. We cannot begin rebuilding containment in the Middle East until we signal that we are leaving Iraq. It is hard to see how else we can diminish the widespread doubts we have created about American imperial ambitions in the region.[3] And assuaging those doubts will be a vital first step to developing successful containment strategies there in the future.

The next step is to deal with Iraq's postwar reconstruction, given the damage that has been wrought on its society and economy. The modern equivalent of a Marshall Plan may be impossible to implement for a long time to come. If the country is wracked by civil war and dysfunctional public institutions, it may be impossible to induce private investment no matter what commitments are forthcoming from the U.S. Treasury.[4] Certainly we must now plan for that possibility by doing what we can to prevent the sectarian conflict from expanding. At a minimum this will require improved relations with Syria and Iran, as well as cooperation with international agencies and other regional powers—not to mention the Europeans. Above all we should avoid uniting potential adversaries by demonizing them as the Bush administration does. The imperative to avoid giving common cause to potential adversaries also means restoring the resolution of the Israel/Palestine conflict to the center of American policy in the region.

We should not become imperialists for democracy, despite Prime Minister Tony Blair's intimations to the contrary.[5] However, we should welcome and support democracy's global spread. Democracy is the best feasible system of government, and we should be on its side except in the rare instances where this is at odds with more pressing priorities of our own national self-defense. Most of the time

promoting democracy abroad is compatible with defending it at home. Indeed, ever since Immanuel Kant thought
he detected a propensity for democracies not to wage war
on one another, political scientists have maintained that
promoting democracy abroad will reduce the hostility that
democracies must confront.[6] Evidence pertinent to definitive evaluation of this claim is controversial and elusive, and
there is some suggestion in the literature that new democracies are particularly prone to be warlike.[7] If the democratic
peace thesis does turn out to be correct, that will stand as a
powerful national security reason for supporting democracy's diffusion around the world.[8]

At a minimum we should avoid supporting repression,
as this fosters breeding grounds and safe havens for extreme
forms of terrorism that will likely come back to haunt us.
Empirical research on the causes of terrorism finds no relationship between deprivations and life chances of individuals and the likelihood that they will themselves engage
in suicide bombing or other forms of extreme terrorism.
However, the same is not true of the communities that tolerate and even support terrorists. Terrorists are unwelcome
in most communities because of the negative fallout that
accompanies their presence—not least the sanctions and
reprisals that communities tolerating them must suffer. It
is when there is widespread repression in communities, as
with the Palestinians on the West Bank, that people become willing to tolerate the risks and costs of harboring
terrorists. As Stathis Kalyvas and Ignacio Sánchez-Cuenca
put it, "What matters is not that the individual personally
experiences political repression or economic deprivation
but, rather, that the living conditions of the community are
so grim and hopeless as to move people to extreme acts."[9]

This finding of the political science literature was vividly brought home to me during a visit to the Qalandia checkpoint in May of 2005. A Palestinian neighborhood between Jerusalem and Ramallah, at that time Qalandia offered a poignant illustration of the daily reality of life under occupation. According to my guide from the Israeli group Women Against the Occupation, Qalandia is a typical West Bank checkpoint. It looks like a giant cattle shed, half the length of a football field. Built of unpainted corrugated iron, it sprawls under the shadow of a concrete guard tower the size of a lighthouse that is pockmarked with bullet holes. The guard tower looms over the infamous mostly completed "Fence"—though here most of it is a massive concrete wall. Bulldozers rumble in the background, clearing its future path. A Palestinian laborer has climbed inside a massive concrete block in search of shade—presumably on a break from manufacturing the instrument of his confinement.

The trip is easy if you are entering Qalandia. Israeli authorities are unconcerned about people going there. You pass unimpeded through a slipway beside the cattle shed— as when walking from the secure zone of an airport back to the check-in area. But my guide double-checks that I really want to go, warning me that the return trip could involve difficulties and might take several hours. Our walk into the town is punctuated by her conversations with various people she is helping whom we meet along the way. A man needs assistance getting medical treatment for a child. Another is caught in an identity-paper mess in the Israeli bureaucracy. The windows and walls around us are speckled with bullet holes from a recent stone-throwing confrontation between Palestinian teenagers and soldiers, during which, apparently, a child was shot. Eventually we refresh ourselves at a café before starting the return journey. Soon I discover why my guide cautioned me about what might lie ahead.

Women and young children are divided from men at the start of the thirty-meter trudge into the elongated shed; they must pass through separate caged turnstiles. The men's line, which is longer, also moves more slowly. A guard looks at my U.S. passport, scratches his head, and waves us to the women's line. As we inch into the shed, the corrugated structure amplifies the dull whine of unhappy children. Everyone ignores the crying: a constant companion about which they can do nothing. The adults shuffle silently forward, their faces blank with tedium. The walk to the turnstile takes half an hour. My guide says the line is moving well today; it sometimes takes hours.

Ahead, a woman holds an infant with one arm and an overstuffed shopping bag with the other. A toddler's anxious fists clutch her skirt as she maneuvers through the turnstile designed for one adult at a time. A wizened old man, who had been sent by a sympathetic soldier to the women's line, is shooed back to the end of the men's line by a different one—his eyes brimming with frustration. Now his wait will be even longer. The stickler for the rules, perhaps a quarter of the old man's age, is impassive. It is striking how young most of the soldiers look—armed children in green fatigues. Were it not for the grimness of the tense dusty spectacle, they could be teenagers playing a game.

Emerging from the turnstile, I discover that a female soldier with a shock of red hair is pointing an M-16 rifle directly at my chest. She is leaning on a table about ten

meters in front of me; I wonder whether it's a safe distance to be from a suicide bomber. Nonchalantly, she chews
gum as her bored eye looks me over. Its barely perceptible
twitch bids me to move forward. Most men must lift their
shirts to show that they are without bomb, but the soldier
recognizes my guide and intuits that we are best let through
with a minimum of fuss. Women Against the Occupation
habitually visit checkpoints armed with cameras and tape
recorders. They seek out confrontations with soldiers that
can make their way into the media. The child-guard waves
me by with a contemptuous—or is it envious?—glance at
my passport.

The humiliation that goes on at these checkpoints has
to be experienced for its full force to be grasped. It reaches
an extreme at Qalandia, which is not even at a border with
Israel; going there means passing at least one more checkpoint. The people you meet on the West Bank believe Qalandia's sole purpose is to harass and humiliate them. Imagine yourself in the place of people who must pass one,
two, or even three such checkpoints in each direction to
and from work every day, and the question is thrown into
sharp relief: why would they *not* support and harbor militias and terrorist groups whose announced purpose is to
relieve them of their plight? As we saw in chapter 5, the
tragic irony is that, absent this kind of humiliating mass repression, popular support for terrorism among Palestinians
on the West Bank would most likely erode.

In mid-2006 Israel's Kadima-led government under Ehud
Olmert signaled its intention to implement the Sharon plan
for a unilateral Israeli withdrawal from the West Bank to
the land behind the Fence. This will leave some 400,000
Jewish settlers there, with the Palestinians hemmed into

disconnected territories that cannot possibly constitute a viable polity or economy. Vast numbers of them will be forced to pass checkpoints every day: sometimes to work in Israel or for the settlers, but just as often to get to their own schools, fields, orchards, and relatives in their Fence-bisected villages and towns. It is scarcely imaginable that implementing Kadima's plan will not produce a third Intifada.

If the United States stands by the Bush administration's position that any settlement must accept new "realities on the ground," at a minimum this will strip any future American administration of the chance to be an honest broker in the Middle East conflict. More likely it will ensure the persistence of a potent breeding ground for terrorism directed at American targets and citizens. Refusing to underwrite oppression by allies we otherwise support should be a nonnegotiable feature of U.S. national security policy. America should stand firmly for a settlement in the Middle East from the Jordan River to the Mediterranean that can garner democratic legitimation from all the populations whose vital interests are affected by it. Anything short of this places our national security at risk unnecessarily.

Refusing to endorse repression, even when engaged in by otherwise democratic allies, is an essential feature of a sound national security strategy, but what of democracy promotion beyond this? Containment supplies the United States with no license to engage in regime toppling at will; it does imply, however, that when democratic movements with indigenous support confront authoritarian regimes, we should support these organic movements. This will be perceived very differently from gratuitous regime change imposed to further a U.S. agenda, as is demonstrated by the contrast between the effects of sanctions in South Africa during the 1980s and those in Iraq during the 1990s.

Sanctions in Iraq were imposed partly to secure Iraqi compliance with the containment regime after 1991, as distinct from promoting regime change. Whether they were necessary or useful for security reasons continues to be debated. It seems clear that they were not well crafted to achieve that goal. As designed, the oil-for-food program invited corruption, as we have seen, and Clinton secretary of state Madeleine Albright has since acknowledged that sanctions could have been more "smart" and narrowly drawn to contain Iraqi aggression.[10] But the Clinton administration was ambiguous between this purpose and the goal of inducing regime change.

If regime change was the goal, Secretary Albright played right into Saddam Hussein's hands by responding to *60 Minutes* reporter Leslie Stahl, when she asked about half a million child deaths resulting from U.S. sanctions in Iraq, "We think the price is worth it."[11] Saddam's virtually unchallenged political monopoly, together with his vicelike control over the media, enabled him to capitalize on such statements, deploying poignant pictures of suffering children on television. In this way he turned the sanctions into propaganda victories about U.S. responsibility for the plight of the Iraqi population, feeding anti-Americanism and deflecting attention from his own repression.

Contrast this with the South African experience. During the 1980s the worldwide antiapartheid movement brought increasing pressure to bear on the United States and other Western governments to impose sanctions. The Reagan administration resisted strongly, partly because they saw South Africa as a strategic ally in the Cold War. They argued that sanctions would harm poor blacks more than they would the white elite, pressing for "constructive engagement" with the apartheid regime instead. But these arguments were undercut by the fact that the African National Congress (ANC) came out in strong support of the sanctions that Congress eventually imposed over President Reagan's veto.[12] The U.S. sanctions became instrumental in buttressing antiapartheid sanctions elsewhere, and fueling the movement for private-sector divestment by pension funds and other major economic players.

How effective sanctions can be at encouraging regime change continues to be debated; current scholarship suggests they can have a mild positive impact.[13] Given this, it makes sense for the United States to be associated with sanctions in the service of regime change only when a significant sector of the indigenous democratic opposition calls for this. Otherwise the United States is likely to be seen as a selfish actor, not a force for progressive democratic change, by the people who must bear the brunt of their impact. It therefore makes sense for the United States to continue to impose sanctions against Burma, as called for by U Maung Maung, general secretary of the Federation of Trade Unions there, and Aung San Su Kyi's National League for Democracy. But sanctions in the service of regime change—as distinct from containment—are a more dubious proposition in North Korea, where the regime derives propaganda benefits from them similar to those derived by Saddam Hussein in Iraq. It is, in any case, doubtful whether Kim Jong-il's regime is vulnerable to external pressure, particularly if the international community is unwilling to stand by and let hundreds of thousands starve in the next famine there.[14]

Deferring to indigenous opposition movements can involve difficult judgment calls. In South Africa, the Inkatha Freedom Party opposed sanctions, but it lacked the ANC's broad-based support. One rule of thumb is to be strongly suspicious of expatriate movements whose leaders claim the mantle of legitimate opposition, particularly when they have exit options that exempt them from paying the costs of being wrong. Whether it is the Cuban expatriates who led President Kennedy into the Bay of Pigs, Ahmed Chalabi's predictions about flowers in the streets of Baghdad, or Michael Ledeen and Manucher Ghorbanifar's insistence that Iran is tottering on the verge of collapse,[15] unless there are demonstrable links to indigenous opposition groups with widespread support, getting behind the agendas of expatriates will likely be ineffective and blow up in our face. Our default posture should be to support indigenous democratic movements and pressure authoritarian regimes to negotiate settlements, not to impose paternalistic decisions in the name of delivering liberation.

This is not to deny that intervention will sometimes be warranted on grounds unrelated to our national security policy. Emergency intervention in genocidal situations such as Rwanda and Darfur will sometimes call for it, as will extreme natural disasters like the tsunami that struck South and Southeast Asia in 2005—though in such cases local governments are usually amenable to it. If we have some chance of being effective, the obligation to intervene will be strong. This will likely involve cooperation with regional powers and international institutions; otherwise we will all too quickly be perceived as Yankee imperialists. That these obligations do not follow from containment is no indictment of it. Rather, it is an acknowledgment that we have international obligations that are unrelated to those that follow from the imperative to protect U.S. national security. Operating as a humanitarian force in the world will not, in any case, harm our national security interests. Particularly in countries with large Muslim populations where the Bush Doctrine has been so costly to America's image,[16] it will be wise for future administrations to engage in activities that can help redress the balance.

There are nonetheless real dangers in trying to turn national security policy into the vehicle for All Good Things, as is evident in one of the few Democratic attempts to come up with an alternative to the Bush Doctrine: "Integrated Power: A National Security Policy for the 21st Century," by Lawrence Korb and Robert Boorstin, published in 2005 by the Center for American Progress—a think tank founded by former Clinton chief of staff John Podesta.[17] Its organizing idea, "Integrated Power," is billed as mobilizing the forces of globalization to respond to fragmented threats that emanate from terrorist groups, extreme regimes, and weak states. Korb and Boorstin make numerous valid criticisms of the Bush Doctrine, but they offer no principled argument in support of their goal of "leading and using alliances to increase the powers of the United States."

Korb and Boorstin's doctrine is as extravagant in its own way as the Bush Doctrine. Their national security policy would commit the United States to preventing conflict around the world regardless of the American interest at stake; to intervening militarily to prevent genocide and ethnic cleansing; to launching a new energy era in the United States; to investing in medical technologies to confront AIDS, tuberculosis, avian flu, and other possible pandemics; to expanding U.S. military manpower; to modernizing international institutions; to reducing the U.S. trade imbalance and the federal deficit while opposing cuts in domestic programs that threaten to "undermine public support for foreign policy programs." They also favor creating a new federal Department for International Development with its own cabinet-level secretary, among other things. This kitchen-sink approach to national security is as unrealistic as it is unappealing. Any politician who adopted "Integrated Power" would be an easy target for political attack.

Generally, containment bids us to support indigenous democratic movements without fighting their battles for them. The menu of possible options, and their costs, is well known: sanctions, divestment, and other forms of international pressure; helping bring deposed dictators to book through the International Criminal Court and other legitimate international tribunals (which would be greatly assisted if the United States recognized their jurisdiction—which currently it does not); material support for democratic resistance movements; and safe harbor for refugees and dissidents. Generalizing about the precise mix of appropriate policies is impossible in the abstract. It depends on difficult judgments about many contingencies: how strong and unified both the regime and the resistance are; what forms of support the resistance is seeking; how likely it is to prevail and to institute democracy if it does prevail; what the chances are that democracy, if instituted, will survive; what the implications of one kind of support rather than another are for other democratic struggles; and many more. *How* the United States should support indigenous democratic movements is a matter for practical judgment. *That* it should support them flows inexorably out of the logic of containment.

Even when support for "friendly" authoritarian regimes does not actually backfire, it erodes American legitimacy. Successive U.S. administrations worked their will in El Salvador and Chile during the 1970s and 1980s, but at the price of convincing many in the developing world that America's widely trumped support for democracy was cynically self-serving. Tortured justifications—like Reagan UN ambassador Jeane Kirkpatrick's attempt to differentiate "authoritarian" pro-Western dictatorships from "totalitarian" procommunist ones—convinced few, if any, other than their proponents. (Ironically in light of subsequent developments, Kirkpatrick held that totalitarian regimes are more stable than authoritarian ones.)[18] For U.S. national security policy to sustain its legitimacy over time, we must not side with oppressors over the oppressed. Precisely because our national security doctrine derives its distinctive justification and moral compass from the democratic ideal, compromising it in the service of other geopolitical goals weakens America's stature abroad. It also undermines support for a unified foreign policy at home, as particular administrations pursue partisan foreign agendas that ignite domestic political conflict and are unlikely to be honored by their successors. The better course is to forge a national security policy that appeals to democratic—rather than liberal, conservative, religious, or secular—values.

We should bear this dictum centrally in mind in dealing with Iran, which promises to be a major security challenge for the United States. The situation is notably harder than it had to be owing to foolish U.S. policies. The Bush administration has contributed mightily here, as we have seen, by spurning Iranian cooperation after 9/11; demonizing the country, thus strengthening its hard-liners and emboldening their nuclear ambitions; being receptive to the voices of expatriates who reinforce American prejudices; and being tone-deaf to the moderates who controlled the Iranian parliament until the conservatives took over at the 2004 election. But there is plenty of blame to go around, going all the way back to the Eisenhower administration. It toppled an elected government in 1953 in favor of the much more pliant shah, who was installed as an American puppet. Additional blame extends through successive administrations up to and including that of President Carter, who unwittingly encouraged the by then hugely unpopular shah and paid the price; the Reagan administration, which backed Iraq in the Iran-Iraq War: and the Clinton administration, which was largely unresponsive to the overtures from President Mohammad Khatami after his election in 1997.

The great tragedy in all this is that Iran, perhaps more than any other Middle Eastern country apart from Israel, has the potential to be a force for Western democratic values. Culturally, many in the population, especially among the young, are strongly pro-Western.[19] There is probably no Middle Eastern country in which there is less interest or investment by the population (as distinct from the present leadership) in the Palestinian-Israeli conflict—not least because the majority of the population are faraway Persians rather than neighboring Arabs who feel they share the humiliation of defeat and loss with Palestinians. Iran is already more democratic than many of its neighbors, despite its ugly oppressive features and structures. It also has the largest Jewish population in the Middle East outside Israel—about twenty-five thousand, with twenty synagogues in Tehran and a constitutional guarantee of a Jewish MP.[20]

Herding Iranians into Huntington's clash-of-civilizations dystopia, which the Bush administration has done at every turn, is the height of folly. Benign neglect would be a vastly more efficacious policy. Just as Kennan recognized that pluralism and competition within the communist world would work to the advantage of the democratic West, we should recognize today that pluralism and competition within the Islamic world—and, indeed, within the Shiite Islamic world—can be expected to do the same. Iran does not and cannot threaten the United States with nuclear weapons. We need to keep our guard up to ensure that this remains the case. Beyond this, the United States should support the democratic forces that emerge in Iran when we can, and leave it alone when we cannot.

Although the United States should not try to weed authoritarian systems out of existence on its own, it should help fledgling democracies survive when it can. The United States should also do what it can to create an environment that is hospitable to democracies that do come into being. It has been evident to political scientists for some time that it is impossible to predict when democratic movements will arise and when they will be successful in overthrowing authoritarian regimes or negotiating democratic settlements with them. There are too many possible paths to democratic success, and those who seek to travel them can be helped along or derailed by too many contingencies to be captured in any useful predictive theory.[21]

The same is not true, however, of the conditions for the survival of democracies. Adam Przeworski and others have found a strong relationship between economic conditions, in particular per capita income, and the likelihood of democratic survival. Democracies appear never to die in wealthy countries, whereas poor democracies are fragile—exceedingly so when annual per capita incomes fall below $2,000 (measured in 1985 dollars). When per capita incomes fall below this threshold, democracies have a one-in-ten chance of collapsing within a year. Between per capita incomes of $2,001 and $5,000 this ratio falls to one-in-sixteen. Above $6,055 annual per capita income, democracies, once established, appear to last indefinitely.[22] Moreover, poor democracies are more likely to survive when governments succeed in generating development and avoiding economic crises.[23]

This suggests that it is wise for the United States to help improve economic conditions in the developing world. It also means adopting economic policies and international aid and debt policies that will alleviate poverty there. Other good reasons exist, to be sure, for working to alleviate global poverty. But the fact that this creates a fertile environment for democracies to survive, if and when they come into being, gives us national security reasons for doing so as well.

7 Our Present Peril

The case for containment, as I have outlined it here, is rooted in the best of America's democratic and national security traditions that the George W. Bush administration spurned. It offers the most feasible basis for protecting Americans and their democracy from violent attack, and can be summarized in the following five national security injunctions:

- Secure America's survival as a democracy into the future.
- Guard against terrorism by containing enabling states, investing in human intelligence, and enhancing homeland security.
- Gear military alliances and collective defense agreements first to America's survival as a democracy and then to the defense of other democracies.
- Support democratic oppositions against dictatorships around the world.
- Sow the seeds of an environment friendly to democracy by promoting economic development in poor countries.

This doctrine is morally superior to the bellicose unilateralism at the core of the Bush administration's recently reiterated *National Security Strategy*. It stands in realistic contrast to their stunning disregard for husbanding military resources, and matching them to genuine threats. Containment can also appeal to the right allies—democratic countries around the world and those seeking to fight for democracy in countries controlled by authoritarian regimes. Containment protects Americans and their democracy, and it commits America's might and moral authority to a global agenda that eschews self-aggrandizement and hegemony in favor of working to create a world that no one can dominate.

The failure on which I have sought to focus attention here is not simply of the Bush administration's national security policy. My motivating concern has been with how the Bush Doctrine filled the vacuum created by the disintegration of the criminal justice approach to terrorism, and what to do about it. That so radical a sea change in national security policy could happen with no serious political debate is remarkable and disturbing. After 9/11 Democrats were shell-shocked like much of the world, while the neoconservatives in the administration seized the moment to put their long-conceived plans into motion.[1] But why has no alternative materialized since? In a healthy democracy arguments like mine would by now be vying with others for the attention of the Bush Doctrine's opponents.

As if to underscore this reality, in November of 2005 conservative House Democrat and decorated war veteran Jack Murtha caused a firestorm by calling for the immediate withdrawal of American troops from Iraq.[2] Republican attempts to discredit him backfired, reflecting the erosion of public support for President Bush's prosecution of the war.[3] But Murtha, who had voted to authorize the invasion and had previously been a vigorous supporter of the war, was in no position to make the case that really needed making: that the Bush Doctrine is fundamentally wrong-headed and needs to be rethought from the ground up. The problem was not flawed execution of a sound strategy, as Murtha's comments suggested. The strategy was unsound to begin with.

The intelligence "failure" over WMD masked larger institutional and political failures on Capitol Hill. In view of what we have since learned of dissenting views within the intelligence community, and field reports that were at variance with the administration's public claims about the threat Iraq actually posed, the questions have to be put: Where were the checks and balances? Where was the loyal opposition? In the absence of a vigorous opposition it is easy for governments to get people to support war. As Hermann Goering put it long ago: "That is easy. All you have to do is to tell them they are being attacked, and denounce the pacifists for lack of patriotism and exposing the country to danger."[4]

There was little evidence here of the ambition counteracting ambition that Madison called for in his defense of the separation of powers in *Federalist* 51.[5] The Senate Select Committee on Intelligence found that administration officials did not exert political pressure on intelligence professionals to distort findings, but it never completed its inquiry into whether officials in the administration mischaracterized intelligence by omitting caveats and dissenting opinions.[6] By now it is incontrovertible that the administration was selective to the point of duplicity. The question is this: why did no one call them on it at the time?

Part of the reason is that congressional leaders were not

in fact given access to the same intelligence as was the administration. They saw what the White House shared—principally the national intelligence estimates (NIEs). They did not see the president's daily intelligence briefings, and they lacked direct access to the national security officials who were reporting up the chain of command to the leaders in the executive branch. They were therefore unaware of the extent of disagreement within the intelligence community, and of numerous daily briefings, starting in the spring of 2002, in which the president was told that the intelligence agencies believed it unlikely that Saddam Hussein would mount any attack on the United States—either directly or working through terrorists. Nor were they aware that while senior administration officials were speaking publicly of Iraq's rekindled nuclear program, the intelligence arms in the Energy and State departments disagreed with other agencies about the intelligence claims on which this stance was based.[7] They were likewise unaware that the administration had received field reports discrediting its claims to have discovered mobile biological laboratories in May of 2003 (claims that were nonetheless repeated by senior officials for many months), or of other skeptical voices within the CIA—backed up by high-level human intelligence—concerning WMD.[8]

But John Kerry was only partly right in complaining in April of 2006 that the Bush administration's case for war was "rooted in deceit."[9] Some of the intelligence shared with Hill leaders such as Kerry did reveal gaps between the administration's public claims and the more doubtful intelligence picture on which they were based. The classified version of the much-debated October 2002 NIE, which *was* shared with congressional leaders, detailed substantial disagreement within intelligence communities on whether Iraq was stockpiling chemical and biological weapons and whether it was reconstituting its nuclear program. Neither these disagreements, nor the significant qualifications and caveats to the NIE's main conclusions about Iraq's illicit weapons programs, appeared in the public version to which the administration appealed in making the case for war.[10]

True, congressional leaders were not allowed to reveal the contents of the classified version of the NIE, but at a minimum it should have made Democrats on the Hill less supine before the administration's war juggernaut. No senator or representative asked publicly whether there was contrary intelligence or disagreement among intelligence professionals, or whether there were field reports suggesting anything different from the findings embraced by the administration. The vote authorizing President Bush to go to war, while not actually a vote for the war, was a blatant attempt by many senators and representatives to duck responsibility in case things went badly—to make sure it was George W. Bush's war. But even among those who opposed the war resolution, no one went public with searching questions about the intelligence. Rather than complaining about cherry picking later, they should have been demanding evidence that cherries were not being picked at the time. Members of Congress were entitled to read the ninety-two-page NIE about Iraq before their October 2002 vote, but no more than six senators and a handful of House members reportedly did so.[11]

Administrations invariably try to control the flow of information so as to minimize opposition to what they want to do; the Bush administration is not special in this regard.

Ronald Reagan's administration kept its arms-for-hostages and Nicaragua funding under wraps in the White House—in violation of the Boland Amendment.[12] The Nixon administration was famously secretive, especially about national security policy.[13] As far back as 1848, in the course of explaining his opposition to the Mexican war, Representative Abraham Lincoln warned against allowing presidents to engage in preventive wars based on their unverified assertions of national peril. They can all too easily make unwise decisions, or act from narrowly political motives like reviving their sagging popularity.[14] There are good reasons to insist on congressional endorsement of all presidential decisions to wage war, but most especially preventive war.

It is the job of the legislative branch, and particularly those in the opposition party, not to play along on trust. Democracies depend for their health and vitality on vigorous contestation of ideas; this is part of what accounts for their institutional superiority over dictatorships. Institutionalized opposition also helps improve the quality of decisions by shining light in dark corners and bringing awkward facts to the surface—holding the government's feet to the fire. Had Kerry and the other Democratic leaders on the Hill been more willing to play these opposition roles, it might have been possible to derail the invasion.

The Democrats' being swept along by the administration's agenda is one of the most palpable costs of their failure to develop an alternative to the Bush Doctrine. This is underscored by the large numbers of Democrats in both houses of Congress who voted to authorize the Iraq invasion,[15] by their inattention to national security doctrine in the 2004 primaries, by the vacuous 2004 Kerry campaign, and by the subsequent attempts to keep the spotlight on the administration's failures rather than to reshape the debate from the ground up. There seem to be three reasons for this Democratic failure.

The first is shock and awe. The attacks of 9/11 turned the Democrats into donkeys in the headlights. They stood by, mesmerized, as the neoconservatives in the Defense Department and the White House moved with alacrity to redefine American national security and the strategy for securing it. But by the time of the Iraq invasion a year and a half later, the Democrats on Capitol Hill were more like a herd of cows being chased across a field by a yapping dog. By then significant dissent was being voiced by traditional international allies in response to the new course being set by the administration. There was also evidence of dissent within the intelligence community, as we have seen, which should have prompted caution had the Democrats been willing to look at that evidence. But they were running scared of a popular president in wartime.

The moral of this story is to keep your head when others around you are panicking. The spring of 2003 was a long way from the next election; a year and a half is a hundred lifetimes in politics. How much better placed would Senator Kerry have been to attack President Bush in the 2004 campaign had he not voted to authorize the war that was by then in such obvious trouble? As it was, he was reduced to oscillating among explaining away his vote, saying he would have prosecuted the war more effectively, and opining he would put 40,000 additional troops into Iraq.[16] Yet if 225,000 troops could not maintain order in a hostile country with a collapsed regime and a population of twenty-five million people, what reason was there to suppose that 265,000 could? If anything, this conjured up the disquieting possibility that a Kerry administration foreign policy might be a replay of the Johnson administration.[17] More than anything, it underscored the reality that Kerry offered no fundamental alternative to the Bush Doctrine.

A second reason for the dearth of alternatives to the Bush Doctrine concerns the discomfort of many on the Democratic left with the whole subject of national security policy. Those who believe that the United States has been a source of great harm and oppression in the world over the past several decades might be reluctant to engage with what U.S. national security strategy should be *now*, lest it somehow tar them with the brush of legitimating the status quo. A strategy for securing America today is all too easily seen as a strategy for securing hegemonic power and ill-gotten gains.

This concern should not be dismissed lightly, not least because ignorance of the harm for which the United States bears responsibility limits our awareness of how malevolent our image is in much of Africa, Asia, and Latin America. But one can grant much of the left critique of American global behavior over the past half century yet still be left with the vital question: and what now? Whatever combination of decisions, forces, and events brought the United States to its present geopolitical position, we still have to choose what our policies will be going forward. That the United States has often failed as a global force for democracy in the past makes all the more urgent the task of coming up with principles and strategies to enable it to be such a force in the future. The lesson to be drawn from the events since 9/11 is that if those who favor progressive democratic change in the world fail to develop a viable national security agenda, others will.

Sometimes it is said that insisting that "you can't beat something with nothing" is belied by American history. After all, FDR made up much of the New Deal as he went along. This is true, and it is possible, no doubt, that a crisis of the proportions of the Great Depression might give the Democrats control of American politics for a generation—particularly if the Republicans are seen as culpable for precipitating that crisis. On a smaller scale, the price in lost support on Capitol Hill that the Bush administration paid in 2006 for its Iraq failures might well give the Democrats a good shot at the White House in 2008.

That possibility cannot be discounted, even if the Democrats fail to develop alternative policies. Predicting the future is fraught with danger, and certainly no one can predict what politics might develop out of a major economic or geopolitical crisis. But Democrats and others who are troubled by the America the Bush Doctrine has wrought would be unwise to count on Republican self-destruction, or being handed the keys to the White House amid a catastrophic crisis. They would do better to take their cue from the neoconservatives who carefully planned their agenda for many years and were ready to advance it, filling the vacuum created by 9/11, when the opportunity presented itself.

A third reason for the Democrats' failure to develop an alternative to the Bush Doctrine requires attention to more than their lack of ideas about national security. It is rooted in their misguided attempt to reinvent themselves since the 1980s at the behest of the Democratic Leadership Council (DLC). The Democratic Party was, to be sure, in need of renewal in the changed post–Cold War circumstances, and their spotty record in presidential politics goes back to the 1950s. But the path they took has been disastrous because it lacks well-articulated moral principles that can be defended as appealing to its natural constituencies. Rather, it rests on the idea of "triangulation." It was bequeathed to them by Republican political consultant Dick Morris, sometime adviser to Bill Clinton and architect of his successful 1996 reelection campaign. The essence of triangulation is to steal your opponents' issues by proposing "lite" versions of their policies—peeling off their moderate supporters while your own base, with little to do but grumble, can be counted on not to defect.[18] President Clinton's embrace of welfare reform in 1996 is often cited as a textbook illustration.[19] On a host of issues President Clinton and DLC candidates have embraced this tactic, refashioning the national Democratic Party in much the same way as Tony Blair refashioned "New Labour" in the United Kingdom.

Triangulation is often given credit for the Democrats' successes since the 1980s, though just what those alleged successes were is difficult to pin down. Bill Clinton was surely an outlier as the most charismatic presidential candidate since John Kennedy, and his election in 1992 was in any case greatly assisted by Ross Perot's presence on the ballot as a third-party candidate. In 1994, the Democrats lost control of the House of Representatives for the first time in a generation and were unable to regain it over the next five elections. The Senate has been in Republican hands for almost all of this time as well. Republicans have also made net gains in control of state legislatures and governorships across the country from the 1970s through 2004.[20] Commitment to DLC policies and strategies did little for Vice President Al Gore in 2000, who managed only to wrestle

George Bush to a draw despite a favorable economic climate for an incumbent and foreign policy not a significant issue.[21] And although John Kerry had his tensions with the Clintons and the DLC in 2004, he did not depart significantly from their triangulating strategies and politics.[22]

Triangulation's central flaw is that it is good tactics but bad strategy. In the short run it can deliver as promised, but as soon as your opponent realizes what you are doing, politics becomes about shifting the goalposts. Newt Gingrich was the consummate genius at this in the 1990s. He effectively "mainstreamed" extreme positions by moving them onto the agenda as the Democrats chased the perpetually vanishing middle ground over the horizon. Repeal of the estate tax is a signal illustration. No one had regarded this as a serious possibility when the Republicans crafted their *Contract with America*—the blueprint for their 1994 insurgency on Capitol Hill. That document proposed only a reform of the tax, and the legislation they introduced in 1995 called for a modest expansion of the exclusion from $600,000 to $750,000 over three years, after which it would have been indexed for inflation. Yet by June 2001—*before* the enhanced legitimacy conferred on President Bush as a result of 9/11—the estate tax was repealed as part of his unprecedented $1.35 trillion tax cut, which was enacted and signed into law in record time. Less than a decade earlier, the Democrats' position had been to favor *cutting* the exclusion to $200,000 in order to fund improvements in Medicare. By 2001 triangulation had induced them to support a $5 million exemption in order to forestall outright repeal. In this they failed, so that the administration achieved repeal with considerable bipartisan support.[23]

Triangulation is self-defeating also because it lacks a principled basis. A triangulating move might peel off enough votes to win in a given race or on a given issue, but in the medium term it is bound to alienate vital supporters. The people who work for campaigns—stuffing envelopes, knocking on doors, staffing phone banks, organizing events—are never going to be satisfied by purely instrumental politics. They want to win, to be sure, but they want to win for a cause they believe is right. The more opportunistic candidates become, the more disheartened will these people be. A great deal of the Republican success in American domestic politics since the 1970s stems from the fact that they have been on a moral crusade for policies that their activists believe are right. Again, the history of estate tax repeal is illuminating. In 1926 an attempt was made to repeal the tax. Proponents argued, much as they would again in the 1990s, that the tax penalized work and saving, and rewarded profligacy. Their opponents countered with moral arguments as well: that America is based on equality of opportunity, not inherited wealth, and that giving rich heirs something for nothing would spoil them. The repeal effort failed. In the 1990s, by contrast, the opponents avoided such arguments, relying instead on appeals to naked interest. "You won't pay it!" was their mantra—as 98 percent of the population would not. Yet they failed to mobilize effective opposition on this basis, underscoring the reality that, to mobilize people for political action, you must present them with a cause that they can believe is right.[24]

This is no less true of national security policy. However misguided the neoconservatives who invented the Bush Doctrine might be, they are on a moral crusade to spread their conception of freedom around the world by utilizing American might. Their doctrine has been decades in the making. Intellectuals like Norman Podhoretz and William Kristol began developing it in the 1970s. It has been marketed for years in signature publications like *Commentary* and the *Weekly Standard*. It has been plied on Capitol Hill and to successive Republican administrations from conservative think tanks like Heritage and the American Enterprise Institute.[25] As with much of the conservative domestic agenda, the response from Democrats has been to ignore it, make fun of it, or at best criticize it—but not to articulate a principled alternative. When George W. Bush came into office in 2000, the neoconservatives found a fully receptive administration in the White House. 9/11 presented a unique opportunity to put their ideas into practice, and they moved with lightning speed. The Democrats were no readier to stop this than they were to derail the tax-cutting locomotive that has driven much of the Republicans' domestic agenda since 2000.[26]

Just as opportunistic parties lose legitimacy at home, opportunistic governments lose it abroad—at least among those who are looking to secure a democratic future. The Bush Doctrine is in one important sense frankly opportunistic. Its proclaimed allegiance to "coalitions of the willing" advertises that anyone will do, no matter how unsavory they might be. When the Bush administration has found it useful to work with authoritarian regimes in its war on terror, this has not been accompanied by any pressure on them to democratize. Indeed, in what is perhaps the height of its cynical opportunism, in 2002 and 2003 the administration was *both* leveling not-so-veiled military threats at Syria *and* sending prisoners there for off-shore interrogation—where U.S. prohibitions against the use of torture would not apply.[27]

Opportunistic as the Bush Doctrine might be in its approach to international alliances, Democrats cannot do better by chasing after Republicans with triangulation—for instance, by temporizing over whether to set a date for departure from Iraq. The war resolution that Senator Kerry supported in 2002 was nothing other than a blank check for the administration.[28] As we saw, it left Kerry stymied when it came to arguing for a principled alternative in his 2004 campaign. It is worth noting, in this regard, that Senator Hillary Clinton, whose celebrity status and vast campaign war chest made her an early favorite for the Democratic nomination in 2008, voted for the same resolution and began busily reinventing herself as a national security hawk after 2004—just as triangulation would dictate.[29] But if a Democratic candidate wins the keys to the White House by triangulating into the Bush Doctrine, what will she or he have won?

And what will America have lost? Rather than focus on short-run electoral tactics that throw practicality and ideals to the wind, aspirants to high political office should take a harder look at strategies that have worked, and that build on America's best democratic and national security traditions. Containment, adapted to the realities of the post-9/11 world, is such a strategy, and, as I have argued in these pages, it offers the most viable hope for securing our people and our democracy into the future. It commits the United States to sensible and sustainable policies around the world. It enables us to promote democracy while avoiding the mantle of imperialism. And it does these things in ways that can restore our government's moral capital and political legitimacy at home and abroad. If forcefully stated and defended, its logic, its realism, and its attractiveness will resonate with Americans—as they have done in the past. That is the case for rebuilding containment.

Acknowledgments

In addition to Jim Brooke's invitation to speak to the Yale Club of Tokyo in September of 2004, the early enthusiasm of my agent, Wendy Strothman, and my publisher, Ian Malcolm, were essential to this book's timely appearance. I presented versions of the evolving manuscript to the Harvard Club of South Africa, to the Political Science Department at El Colegio de México in Mexico City, in a discussion with parliamentary members of the Democratic Party of Japan, as a lecture in the Company of Scholars series at Yale, and at a conference on philosophy and the social sciences at Villa Lanna, Prague. Useful comments were received in all these venues.

Variants of the manuscript have been read, in part or whole, by Bruce Ackerman, Vahid Alaghband, Iradj Bagherzade, Robert Dahl, Peter Dougherty, Michael Doyle, Anoush Ehteshami, John Lewis Gaddis, Michael Graetz, Clarissa Hayward, Richard Kane, Robert Lane, Ellen Lust-Okar, Ian Malcolm, David Mayhew, Shaul Mishal, Nicoli Nattrass, John Roemer, Frances Rosenbluth, Pierre Schmidt, Jeremy Seekings, Peter Swenson, Ernesto Zedillo, and three anonymous readers for Princeton University Press. I am grateful for the many helpful suggestions I have received, some of which have been heeded. The usual caveats apply.

Mina Alaghband, Ian Carroll, Andrew Iliff, Paul Kellogg, Jeffrey Mueller, and Larry Wise all provided outstanding research assistance at different stages during the book's writing. I am deeply grateful to them, and to the Institution for Social and Policy Studies, the MacMillan Center, and the Provost at Yale for the research support that enabled me to employ them. This list of acknowledgments would be incomplete if it did not record my profound thanks for the superb editing of Lauren Lepow.

Notes

Preface

1. This story is recounted in Michael Graetz and Ian Shapiro, *Death by a Thousand Cuts: The Fight over Taxing Inherited Wealth* (Princeton: Princeton University Press, 2005).

2. "Gore Accepts Democratic Nomination as 'My Own Man,'" CNN.com, August 18, 2000, http://transcripts.cnn.com/2000/ALLPOLITICS/stories/08/17/gore.speech/index.html [8/2/06].

3. *The National Security Strategy of the United States of America* (Washington, DC: The White House, 2002), http://www.whitehouse.gov/nsc/nss/2002/index.html [8/2/06], and *The National Security Strategy of the United States of America* (Washington, DC: The White House, 2006), http://www.whitehouse.gov/nsc/nss/2006/index.html [8/2/06].

4. See "Transcript: First Presidential Debate," Coral Gables, FL, September 30, 2004, http://www.washingtonpost.com/wp-srv/politics/debatereferee/debate_0930.html [8/2/06]; and "Kerry's Top Ten Flip Flops," *CBS News*, September 29, 2004 [8/2/04], http://www.cbsnews.com/stories/2004/09/29/politics/main646435.shtml [8/1/06].

5. Nicholas Sambanis, "It's Official: There Is Now a Civil War in Iraq," *New York Times*, July 23, 2006, p. A13.

6. Leader, *Economist*, August 13, 2005, pp. 12–13.

7. Rory Stewart, "Even in Iraq, All Politics Is Local," *New York Times*, July 13, 2006, p. A23.

Chapter 1
The Idea Vacuum

1. *The National Security Strategy of the United States of America* (Washington, DC: The White House, 2002), http://www.whitehouse.gov/nsc/nss.html [8/1/05].

2. In 1825 Adams was put into office by the House of Representatives despite his having lost the popular vote to Andrew Jackson the previous year (when neither had won a majority of electoral college votes). This was widely believed to have been the result of a corrupt bargain between Adams and the fourth-place finisher, Henry Clay, in return for which Clay became Adams's secretary of state. "Adams, John Quincy," *Encyclopædia Britannica Online*, http://search.eb.com/eb/article-136 [6/20/06].

3. Republicans gained two seats in the Senate and eight seats in the House in 2002. In 2004, they gained two more House seats and four senators.

4. See the second Bush-Kerry presidential debate, 10/08/04, Washington University, St. Louis, MO, www.debates.org/pages/trans2004c.html [10/5/05].

5. Michael Dukakis 1988 nomination acceptance speech, July 21, 1988, http://www.geocities.com/Wellesley/1116/dukakis88.html [10/5/05].

6. X, "The Sources of Soviet Conduct," *Foreign Affairs*, July 1947, www.foreignaffairs.org/19470701faessay25403-p0/x/the-sources-of-soviet-conduct.html [10/12/05].

7. Kennan opposed the formation of NATO on the grounds that it would militarize the confrontation with the USSR unnecessarily. Certainly it solidified the confrontation with COMECON. Whether the Cold War would have been won by containment alone, without NATO and the concomitant rearmament of Europe, is an open question that we need not settle here, since my version of containment does not rule out such alliances.

Chapter 2
End of the Criminal Justice Consensus

1. See "Millennium Bomber Sentenced to 22 Years," http://www.elitestv.com/pub/2005/Jul/EEN42e7f6cb3616e.ht ml [7/28/05].

2. "Bush had never seen the plan [to eliminate al Qaeda], the pieces of which had first been briefed to Cheney, Rice, Powell, and others on his team in January. I had not been allowed to brief the President on terrorism in January or since, not until today, September 11. It had taken since January to get the Cabinet-level meeting that I requested 'urgently' within days of the inauguration to approve an aggressive plan to go after al Qaeda. The meeting had finally happened exactly one week earlier, on September 4." Richard Clarke, *Against All Enemies: Inside America's War on Terror* (New York: Free Press, 2004), p. 26.

3. Promotion of National Unity and Reconciliation Act, 1995, 20 (1) b, p. 12. http://www.info.gov.za/acts/1995/a34-95 .pdf [11/15/05].

4. The fourth plane, which crashed into a rural field near Shanksville, Pennsylvania, following passenger resistance, had apparently been intended for the White House.

5. United Nations Security Council Resolution 1333, adopted December 19, 2000, http://daccessdds.un.org/doc/UN DOC/GEN/N00/806/62/PDF/N0080662.pdf?OpenElement [10/31/05].

6. Chapter VII, Article 51, of the United Nations Charter provides, inter alia, that "[n]othing in the present Charter shall impair the inherent right of individual or collective self-defense if an armed attack occurs against a member of the United Nations, until the Security Council has taken the measures necessary to maintain international peace and security. Measures taken by members in the exercise of this right of self-defense shall be immediately reported to the Security Council." http://www .un.org/aboutun/charter/chapter7.htm [10/31/05].

Chapter 3
Filling the Vacuum

1. See Samuel Huntington, *The Clash of Civilizations and the Remaking of World Order* (New York: Simon & Schuster, 1998). On "Islamofascism," see right-wing talk-show host Michael Savage's *Liberalism Is a Mental Disorder* (Nashville, TN: Nelson Current, 2005).

2. See http://www.rightwingnews.com/quotes/bushquotes.php [8/1/05]. It was not until October 2005 that President Bush began to refer to the war on militant Islam. "Some call this evil Islamic radicalism; others, militant Jihadism; still others, Islamo-fascism." See President Bush's Address at the National Endowment for Democracy, October 6, 2005, http://www.whitehouse.gov/news/releases/2005/10/20051006-3.html [6/14/06].

3. The State of the Union, January 29, 2001, http://www.whitehouse.gov/news/releases/2002/01/20020129-11.html [7/22/05].

4. http://www.whitehouse.gov/news/releases/2002/06/20020601-3.html [7/22/05].

5. "In Cheney's Words: The Administration Case for Removing Saddam Hussein," *New York Times*, August 27, 2002, p. A8.

6. *The National Security Strategy of the United States* (2002), p. 13, http://www.whitehouse.gov/nsc/nss5.html [7/22/05].

7. Ibid., p. 15.

8. Ibid., p. 5.

9. "Cheney Calls Confronting Iraq 'Crucial' to War against Terror," quoting Cheney's January 30, 2003, speech to the Thirtieth Annual Conservative Political Action Conference in Arlington, Virginia, http://www.useu.be/Terrorism/USResponse/Jan3003CheneyTerrorism.html [7/25/05].

10. Donald Rumsfeld, "Taking the Fight to the Terrorists Is the Right Tactic," *Stars and Stripes*, October 29, 2003.

11. See *The National Security Strategy of the United States*

(2006), p. 3, http://www.whitehouse.gov/nsc/nss/2006/index .html [9/8/06].

12. See http://usinfo.state.gov/usa/infousa/facts/democrac/ 50.htm [7/27/05].

13. See Dexter Perkins, *History of the Monroe Doctrine* (Boston: Little Brown & Co., 1963), and Ernest R. May, *The Making of the Monroe Doctrine* (Cambridge, MA: Harvard University Press, Belknap Press, 1975).

14. *The National Security Strategy of the United States* (2002), p. 6, http://www.whitehouse.gov/nsc/nss3.html [7/28/05].

15. NATO is supposed to be a purely defensive alliance. In this case it attacked a country that was not threatening any NATO member. Instability in the Balkans was cited as a direct threat to the security interests of their members, and the intervention was also defended as needed owing to an "international humanitarian emergency." But the action was not supported by the UN, where the Russians and the Chinese would have vetoed any Security Council resolution. The action would have sparked more opposition than it did in the Middle East had NATO not been intervening on the side of Muslims. See, for example, Victor T. Le Vine, "Mideast Cautiously Supports NATO in Kosovo," *St. Louis Post-Dispatch*, May 3, 1999, and Allan Thompson, "Jordan Backs NATO, Canada," *Toronto Star*, March 14, 1999.

16. *The National Security Strategy of the United States* (2002), p. 6, http://www.whitehouse.gov/nsc/nss3.html [7/27/05].

17. Ibid., p. vi.

18. "You Are Either with Us or against Us," CNN.com, November 6, 2001, http://archives.cnn.com/2001/US/11/06/ gen.attack.on.terror/ [7/27/05].

19. Scott A. Silverstone, "The Ethical Limits to Preventive War," Carnegie Council, May 2004, http://www.cceia.org/ viewMedia.php/prmID/5108 [7/23/06].

20. NSC: 68 United States Objectives and Programs for Na-

tional Security (April 14, 1950), §VIII C, http://www.mtholyoke
.edu/acad/intrel/nsc-68/nsc68-3.htm [7/23/06].

21. *The National Security Strategy of the United States* (2002),
p. 15, http://www.whitehouse.gov/nsc/nss5.html [7/28/05].

22. Ibid., p. v.

23. *The National Security Strategy of the United States* (2006),
p. 23, http://www.whitehouse.gov/nsc/nss/2006/index.html
[9/8/06].

24. *The National Security Strategy of the United States* (2002),
p. 15, http://www.whitehouse.gov/nsc/nss5.html [7/27/05].

25. Colin Powell, Address to the UN Security Council,
February 5, 2003, http://www.whitehouse.gov/news/releases/
2003/02/20030205-1.html [7/29/05].

26. Asked by Barbara Walters whether he felt the UN pre-
sentation would tarnish his reputation, Powell replied: "Of
course it will. It's a blot. I'm the one who presented it on behalf
of the United States to the world, and [it] will always be a part
of my record. It was painful. It's painful now. . . . There were
some people in the intelligence community who knew at that
time that some of these sources were not good, and shouldn't be
relied upon, and they didn't speak up. That devastated me."
"Powell Calls UN Speech a 'Blot' on His Record," *ABC News*,
http://aolsvc.news.aol.com/news/article.adp?id=200509082317
09990004 [11/14/05].

27. See "Bush Watch War Lies," http://bushwatch.org/wmd
.htm [7/28/05], and "Was the Threat Imminent, Immediate, or
Mortal?" http://zfacts.com/p/559.html [7/28/05].

28. Wendy Ross, "Bush Discusses Future Needs of US
Military with Top Advisers," http://japan.usembassy.gov/e/p/
tp-se1619.html [7/29/05].

29. *The National Security Strategy of the United States* (2002),
p. v, http://www.whitehouse.gov/nsc/nssintro.html [7/29/05].

30. *The National Security Strategy of the United States* (2006), p. 3,
http://www.whitehouse.gov/nsc/nss/2006/index.html [9/8/06].

31. See Terry Neal, "Iraq Fighting Shifts to US Soil," *Washington Post*, November 17, 2005, http://www.washingtonpost.com/wp-dyn/content/article/2005/11/17/AR2005111700651.html [11/22/05].

32. Project for the New American Century, "Open Letter to the President," January 26, 1998, http://www.theindyvoice.com/index.blog?entry_id=417960 [6/16/06]. "Open Letter to the President," February 19, 1998, http://www.iraqwatch.org/perspectives/rumsfeld-openletter.htm [6/16/06].

33. See Sarah Graham-Brown and Chris Toensing, "Why Another War: A Backgrounder on the Iraq Crisis, Middle East Research and Information Project" (October 2002), pp. 10–11, http://www.merip.org/iraq_backgrounder_102202/iraq_bckground_merip_screes.pdf [11/21/05].

34. See David Frum and Richard Perle, *An End to Evil: How to Win the War on Terror* (New York: Random House, 2003), p. 98.

35. Woodrow Wilson, *War Messages*, 65th Cong., 1st Sess., Senate Doc. No. 5, Serial No. 7264, Washington, DC, 1917.

36. Harry Truman, Address before a Joint Session of Congress, March 12, 1947, http://www.yale.edu/lawweb/avalon/trudoc.htm [4/12/06].

37. *The National Security Strategy of the United States* (2002), p. iv, http://www.whitehouse.gov/nsc/nssintro.html [7/29/05].

38. "Bush: World Is Changing for Better," CNN.com, January 21, 2004, http://edition.cnn.com/2004/ALLPOLITICS/01/20/sotu.international/ [7/29/05].

39. In January of that year the Pentagon declared that the search for WMD and nuclear weapons had been abandoned the previous month. Dafna Linzer, "Search for Banned Weapons in Iraq Ended Last Month," http://www.washingtonpost.com/wp-dyn/articles/A2129-2005Jan11.html [7/29/05].

40. "Bush: World Is Changing for Better," CNN.com, January 21, 2004, http://edition.cnn.com/2004/ALLPOLITICS/01/20/sotu.international/ [7/29/05].

41. See http://www.debates.org/pages/trans2000a.html [8/1/05].

42. See ibid.

43. By mid-June of 2006, 2,501 U.S. military had been killed in Iraq since the start of the war. Since January of that year they had been dying at an average rate of 65 per month. See http://icasualties.org/oif/. At that pace the total would be expected to rise to 2,776 by November 2006, 215 more than the 2,551 civilians killed in the 9/11 attacks. See http://www.rand.org/news/press.04/11.08b.html [6/19/06].

44. For one early shot across the bows, see Patrick J. Buchanan, *Where the Right Went Wrong: How Neoconservatives Subverted the Reagan Revolution and Hijacked the Bush Presidency* (New York: Thomas Dunne, 2004).

45. See Christopher Hitchens, "Machiavelli in Mesopotamia," "Prevention and Pre-Emption," and "Regime Change," on www.slate.com [9/8/06]; Paul Berman, "Resolved," *New Republic*, March 3, 2003, and *Terror and Liberalism* (New York: W. W. Norton, 2003).

46. See http://www.rightwingnews.com/quotes/bushquotes.php [8/1/05].

47. See ibid.

48. "You Are Either with Us or against Us," CNN.com, November 6, 2001, http://archives.cnn.com/2001/US/11/06/gen.attack.on.terror/ [7/31/05].

49. http://www.whitehouse.gov/news/releases/2001/11/20011106-2.html [7/31/05].

50. *The National Security Strategy of the United States* (2006), p. 7, http://www.whitehouse.gov/nsc/nss/2006/index.html [9/8/06].

51. See http://www.debates.org/pages/trans2000b.html [8/1/05].

52. See http://lawofwar.org/hague_v.htm [7/31/05].

53. See http://www.infoplease.com/ce6/history/A0835328.html [7/31/05].

54. In a speech in June of 1955 Dulles outraged leaders of the nonaligned nations with his comment that "neutrality has increasingly become obsolete and except under very exceptional circumstances, it is an immoral and shortsighted conception." *Encyclopedia Beta*, http://experts.about.com/e/j/jo/John_Foster_ Dulles.htm [7/23/06].

55. The change was made by the Committee on House Administration at the behest of two Republican congressmen— Bob Ney of Ohio and Walter Jones of North Carolina—following France's refusal to support the U.S. invasion of Iraq in March of 2003. See http://www.cnn.com/2003/ALLPOLITICS/03/11/ sprj.irq.fries/ [8/1/05].

56. See http://www.cbsnews.com/stories/2003/08/26/ politics/main570110.shtml [7/31/05].

57. See http://www.ciaonet.org/special_section/iraq_review/ pi_gov/pi_gov_03.html [8/1/05].

58. *The National Security Strategy of the United States* (2002), p. iv, http://www.whitehouse.gov/nsc/nssintro.html [7/30/05].

59. http://multimedia.belointeractive.com/attack/bush/ 1109bushtext.html [7/31/05].

60. As Dick Cheney put it on NBC's *Meet the Press* in May of 2002: "The prospects of a future attack against the United States are almost certain. Not a matter of if, but when." Mike Allen, *Washington Post*, May 20, 2002, p. A1. "We do know that terrorists are still out there. We know they're trying to plot to launch another attack against the United States." Dick Cheney, Town Hall Meeting, Oregon City, Oregon, September 17, 2004, http://www .whitehouse.gov/news/releases/2004/09/20040917-15.html [7/13/2006].

61. Max Weber famously defined a state as "a human community that (successfully) claims the *monopoly of the legitimate use of physical force* within a given territory." "Politics as a Vocation," in *The Vocation Lectures*, ed. David Owen and Tracy Strong (Indianapolis: Hackett, 2004), p. 33.

Chapter 4
Containment for Democracy

1. Kennan thought that key aspects of containment had been compromised during the last years of the Truman administration. He opposed as counterproductive for containing the Soviets the Truman administration's major foreign policy choices after 1948: the creation of NATO, the decisions to create an independent West Germany and to retain U.S. forces in postoccupation Japan, and the development of the hydrogen bomb. See John Gaddis, *Strategies of Containment*, 2nd ed. (New York: Oxford University Press, 2005), pp. 69–86. The Vietnam War struck him as a disastrous perversion of the doctrine, and he was equivocal, at best, about the Reagan administration's understanding of containment (p. 377). Kennan was uncompromising in his condemnation of the Bush Doctrine in the last years of his life, and of the Democrats for failing to oppose it. See Albert Eisele, *Hill Profile*, The Hill, September 28, 2002, www.mtholyoke.edu/acad/intrel/bush/kennan.htm [10/10/05].

2. Gaddis, *Strategies of Containment*, p. 55.

3. See J.G.A. Pocock, *The Machiavellian Moment: Florentine Political Thought and the Atlantic Republican Tradition* (Princeton: Princeton University Press, 2003).

4. X, "The Sources of Soviet Conduct," *Foreign Affairs*, July 1947, www.foreignaffairs.org/19470701faessay25403-p0/x/the-sources-of-soviet-conduct.html [10/12/05].

5. Gaddis, *Strategies of Containment*, p. 55.

6. Ibid., pp. 272–306. Thus while Kennan ran the Policy Planning Staff, they endorsed the idea of supporting Titoism on the grounds that the Russians feared it "above everything else." See *Foreign Relations of the United States 1949*, vol. 5, *Eastern Europe; The Soviet Union* (Washington, DC: U.S. Government Printing Office, 1976), pp. 9–10.

7. NSC 58, September 14, 1949. Reproduced in Thomas

Etzold and John Lewis Gaddis, *Containment: Documents on American Policy and Strategy* (New York: Columbia University Press, 1978), p. 220.

8. Ibid., pp. 245–46.

9. Niccolò Machiavelli, *The Discourses* (ca. 1517), trans. Leslie J. Walker (Harmondsworth: Penguin, 1979), §1.5.

10. See Ian Shapiro, *Democratic Justice* (New Haven: Yale University Press, 1999), pp. 1–63.

11. "As a new Congress gathers, all of us in the elected branches of government share a great privilege: We've been placed in office by the votes of the people we serve. And tonight that is a privilege we share with newly-elected leaders of Afghanistan, the Palestinian Territories, Ukraine, and a free and sovereign Iraq." President George W. Bush, State of the Union Address, February 2, 2005, http://www.whitehouse.gov/news/releases/2005/02/20050202-11.html [9/8/05].

12. Francis Fukuyama, *America at the Crossroads: Democracy, Power and the Neoconservative Legacy* (New Haven: Yale University Press, 2006); Patrick J. Buchanan, *Where the Right Went Wrong: How Neoconservatives Subverted the Reagan Revolution and Hijacked the Bush Presidency* (New York: Thomas Dunne, 2005).

13. "No people ever was and remained free, but because it was determined to be so; because neither its rulers nor any other party in the nation could compel it to be otherwise. If a people—especially one whose freedom has not yet become prescriptive—does not value it sufficiently to fight for it, and maintains it against any force which can be mustered *within* the country . . . it is only a question in how few years or months that people will be enslaved." John Stuart Mill, "A Few Words on Non-Intervention," in *Essays on Politics and Culture*, ed. Gertrude Himmelfarb (New York: Anchor Books, 1963), pp. 381–82 (Mill's emphasis). For a useful discussion of Mill's views in relation to contemporary debates about foreign intervention, see Michael W. Doyle, "Sovereignty, Humanitarian Intervention, and

Multilateral Substitution" (paper presented at conference, Normative and Empirical Evaluations of Global Governance, Princeton University, February 16–18, 2006).

14. A Gallup poll conducted in Baghdad in August and September 2003, found that 43 percent of respondents believed that U.S. and British forces invaded because of Iraq's oil. Other Baghdad residents cited strategic considerations: "14% said the action was intended to colonize and occupy a portion of the Middle East, and 6% said the motivation was a desire to change the 'map' of the Middle East in a way more attuned to U.S. and Israeli interests." Richard Burkholder, "Baghdadis Gauge U.S. Intent," Subscriber Report: *The 2003 Gallup Poll of Baghdad*, p. 33. In October 2003, a poll conducted by the Iraq Center for Research and Strategic Studies, and commissioned by the International Republican Institute, found that 66.6 percent of Iraqis viewed the coalition forces "as occupying forces," up from 45.9 percent when the coalition forces first arrived. Poll results available online at http://www.iri.org/pdfs/iraq_poll_3.pdf [11/9/05].

15. Listen to Defense Secretary Dick Cheney's prescient words in April 1991: "If you're going to go in and try to topple Saddam Hussein, you have to go to Baghdad. Once you've got Baghdad, it's not clear what you do with it. It's not clear what kind of government you would put in place of the one that's currently there now. Is it going to be a Shia regime, a Sunni regime or a Kurdish regime? Or one that tilts toward the Baathists, or one that tilts toward the Islamic fundamentalists? How much credibility is that government going to have if it's set up by the United States military when it's there? How long does the United States military have to stay to protect the people that sign on for that government, and what happens to it once we leave?" See "Echoes from the Past," The History News Network, http://hnn.us/articles/631.html [11/21/05].

16. See Ian Shapiro, *The State of Democratic Theory* (Princeton: Princeton University Press, 2003), pp. 79–100.

17. Fukuyama, *America at the Crossroads.*

18. See the open letter to President Clinton published by the neoconservative Project for the New American Century on January 26, 1998, at http://www.theindyvoice.com/index .blog?entry_id=417960 [3/24/06].

19. Fukuyama, *America at the Crossroads*, p. 172.

20. Ibid.

21. "The Parties agree that an armed attack against one or more of them in Europe or North America shall be considered an attack against them all and consequently they agree that, if such an armed attack occurs, each of them, in exercise of the right of individual or collective self-defence recognised by Article 51 of the Charter of the United Nations, will assist the Party or Parties so attacked by taking forthwith, individually and in concert with the other Parties, such action as it deems necessary, including the use of armed force, to restore and maintain the security of the North Atlantic area." Article 5 of the North Atlantic Treaty.

22. Vance Serchuk, "Dutch Retreat? The Perils of Turning Afghanistan over to NATO," American Enterprise Institute, January 9, 2006, http://www.aei.org/publications/pubID.23651/pub_ detail.asp [6/18/06].

23. This was despite the fact that Paul Nitze and the other authors of NSC-68 advanced a more aggressively militarized version of containment than Kennan was willing to endorse. See David Mayers, *George Kennan and the Dilemmas of US Foreign Policy* (New York: Oxford University Press, 1988), p. 134.

24. By 2005, overwhelming majorities of Jordanians, Syrians, and Egyptians, as well as Palestinians, had strongly negative views of the United States. See "Revisiting the Arab Street: Research from Within," Center for Strategic Studies, University of Jordan, February 2005, p. 14, http://www.css-jordan.org/new/ REVISITINGTTHEARABSTREETReport.pdf [7/31/06].

25. In 2005, 43 percent of the French population had a favorable attitude toward the United States, down from 63 percent in

2002. http://pewglobal.org/reports/pdf/247france.pdf [7/31/06].
The drop in Germany for the same years was from 61 percent
to 41 percent. http://pewglobal.org/reports/pdf/247germany.pdf
[7/31/06].

26. Nick Paton Walsh and Patrick Wintour, "Putin:
Don't Lecture Me about Democracy," *Observer*, July 16, 2006,
http://observer.guardian.co.uk/world/story/0,,1821488,00.html
[7/26/06].

27. Fukuyama, *America at the Crossroads*, p. 173.

28. See John Rawls, *Political Liberalism* (New York: Columbia University Press, 1993), pp. 131–254.

29. This was the main subject of his famous eight-thousand-
word "Long Telegram" when he was a diplomat in Moscow in
1946 that first got the attention of the Truman administration.

30. See Samuel P. Huntington, *The Clash of Civilizations and
the Remaking of World Order* (New York: Simon and Schuster,
1998).

31. "Americans are asking, why do they hate us? They hate
what we see right here in this chamber—a democratically elected
government. Their leaders are self-appointed. They hate our
freedoms—our freedom of religion, our freedom of speech, our
freedom to vote and assemble and disagree with each other."
George W. Bush, Address to a Joint Session of Congress and the
American People, September 20, 2001, http://www.whitehouse
.gov/news/releases/2001/09/20010920-8.html [9/8/06]. President Bush also commented after the 2004 Madrid bombings,
"These people kill because they hate freedom and they hate what
Spain stands for." George W. Bush, Interview by Television of
Spain, March 12, 2004, http://63.161.169.137/news/releases/
2004/03/20040312-19.html [6/5/04].

32. See President Bush's Address at the National Endowment for Democracy, October 6, 2005, http://www.whitehouse.
gov/news/releases/2005/10/20051006-3.html [6/18/06]. Bush
continued to deny it was intrinsic to the Islamic religion, but,

as with mentioning Iraq in the same paragraph as 9/11 while denying that he was asserting they were connected, the likely result—and perhaps even the intent—was manifest.

33. David Frum and Richard Perle, *An End to Evil: How to Win the War on Terror* (New York: Random House, 2003), p. 42.

34. See Stephen Hopgood, "Tamil Tigers," in *Making Sense of Suicide Missions*, ed. Diego Gambetta (Oxford: Oxford University Press, 2005), pp. 43–76; Robert Pape, *Dying to Win: The Strategic Logic of Suicide Terrorism* (New York: Random House, 2005); and Mia Bloom, *Dying to Kill: The Allure of Suicide Terror* (New York: Columbia University Press, 2005).

35. The definitive treatment of this subject is former intelligence officer Michael Scheuer's *Imperial Hubris: Why the West Is Losing the War on Terror* (Dulles, VA: Potomac Books, 2004).

36. "Iran, Its Neighbours and the Regional Crises," ed. Robert Lowe and Claire Spencer, The Royal Institute of International Affairs, Chatham House, London, 2006, p. 6.

37. Kenneth M. Pollack, *The Persian Puzzle: The Conflict between Iran and America* (New York: Random House, 2004), p. 352.

38. At the time Syria, which was also cooperating with the United States, was restricting the flow of weapons to Hezbollah through Damascus. The Iranian weapons might have been destined for them. Ibid., p. 351.

39. See Bob Woodward, *Plan of Attack* (New York: Simon & Schuster, 2004), pp. 86–89.

40. In 2005 he would be appointed by Kofi Annan to his Alliance of Civilizations, a group dedicated to combating extremism and overcoming cultural barriers between the Western and Muslim worlds.

41. See Anoushiravan Ehteshami, "Iran's International Posture after the Fall of Baghdad," *Middle East Journal* 58, no. 2 (Spring 2004): 180; Jared A. Cohen and Abbas Milani, "The Passive Revolution," *Hoover Digest*, no. 3 (Fall 2005), http://www

.hooverdigest.org/053/cohen.html [6/20/06]. Systematic evidence is difficult to come by, but anecdotal evidence suggests that there continue to be reformist sympathies in the population. After the conservative takeover of Parliament in June of 2005, a reformist rally in Tehran Stadium drew thousands of supporters. Laura Secor, "Fugitives," *New Yorker*, November 21, 2005, and Norman Solomon, "A Threat to Iran's Theocrats and US Neocons: Iran's Growing Reform Movement," Counterpunch.org, June 15, 2005, http://www.counterpunch.org/solomon06152005 .html [6/14/06].

42. Ehteshami, "Iran's International Posture," p. 182.

43. Lowe and Spencer, "Iran, Its Neighbours and the Regional Crises," p. 10.

44. Ehteshami, "Iran's International Posture," p. 183.

45. Ibid., p. 187.

46. "Threats and Responses; Excerpts from Debate on Senate Floor on Use of Force against Iraq," *New York Times*, October 8, 2002, p. A14.

47. "Threats and Responses; Bush's Speech on Iraq: 'Saddam Hussein and His Sons Must Leave,' " *New York Times*, March 18, 2003, p. A14.

48. Hitler's new order "was a force with which we could never have lived at peace, a force which if successful could have come to dominate the eastern power center, too. To have mobilized those two forces together in this way would have been just about as dangerous to us, perhaps not quite, as though it had been the other way around and the Russians had come into possession of the West." Kennan, National War College lecture, September 17, 1948, Kennan Papers, Box 17. Cited in Gaddis, *Strategies of Containment*, p. 32.

49. "On Iraq: Testimony as Delivered by Deputy Secretary of Defense Paul Wolfowitz, and Director, Office of Management and Budget, Joshua Bolten, and Acting Chief of Staff, U.S. Army, General John Keane, Tuesday, July 29, 2003." As Senator Diane Fein-

stein noted, this amounted to $2.5 billion per year. See http://www.defenselink.mil/speeches/2003/sp20030729-depsecdef0385.html [11/15/05].

50. "Since September 2001, the Congress and the President have provided about $323 billion in appropriations for military operations in Iraq and Afghanistan and for other Department of Defense activities in support of the war on terrorism." The Congressional Budget Office, *The Budget and Economic Outlook: Fiscal Years 2007 to 2016* (January 2006), http://www.cbo.gov/ftpdocs/70xx/doc7027/01-26-BudgetOutlook.pdf#page=26 [6/18/06]. Of the 2005 DoD obligation of $83.6 billion, 85 percent was dedicated to Operation Iraqi Freedom.

51. In 2002, William Nordhaus estimated the range as between $121 billion in a "short and favorable" scenario and $1.6 trillion "if the war drags on, occupation is lengthy, nation building is costly, the war destroys a large part of Iraq's oil infrastructure, there is lingering military and political resistance to U.S. occupation in the Islamic world, and there are major adverse psychological reactions to the conflict." "The Economic Consequences of a War with Iraq," *New York Review of Books*, December 5, 2002, http://www.nybooks.com/articles/15850 [6/17/06]. In January of 2006 Linda Bilmes and Joseph Stiglitz put the purely budgetary costs to the taxpayer in the $750 billion to $1.2 trillion range "assuming that the US begins to withdraw troops in 2006 and maintains a diminishing presence for the next five years." "The Economic Costs of the Iraq War: An Appraisal Three Years after the Beginning of the Conflict," http://www2.gsb.columbia.edu/faculty/jstiglitz/cost_of_war_in_iraq.pdf [6/17/06].

52. Kenneth M. Pollack, *The Threatening Storm: The Case for Invading Iraq* (New York: Random House, 2002), pp. xv–xxiv, and Steven Davis, Kevin Murphy, and Robert Topel, "War in Iraq versus Containment," National Bureau of Economic Research working paper #12092 (2006).

53. "Every one, as he is bound to preserve himself, and not to quit his station willfully, so by the like reason, when his own preservation comes not in competition, ought he, as much as he can, to preserve the rest of mankind." John Locke, *Second Treatise of Government*, in *Two Treatises of Government and a Letter Concerning Toleration*, ed. Ian Shapiro (New Haven: Yale University Press, 2003), chap. 2, §6, p. 102.

54. The U.S. alliance with the warlords in Afghanistan to defeat the Taliban was equally a case of realistic compromise, with equally significant long-run costs. These will be difficult to minimize unless a viable Afghan state can be built.

55. Israel is the only recipient of U.S. foreign aid that need not provide regular accounting of how aid is spent. This makes it impossible to police a prohibition on using U.S. funds to underwrite the settlement policy. See Clyde R. Mark, "Israel: U.S. Foreign Assistance," Issue Brief for Congress (Washington, DC: Congressional Research Service, April 26, 2005), pp. 8–9, http://fpc .state.gov/documents/organization/47088.pdf [6/20/06].

56. See President Bush's joint White House press conference with Ariel Sharon, April 14, 2004, at http://www.whitehouse .gov/news/releases/2004/04/20040414-4.html [4/3/06].

57. "President George W. Bush's endorsement of Ariel Sharon's policies has mostly hurt one important group—moderate Arabs. The new US position received extremely angry reactions from Middle East leaders and activists." Daoud Kuttab, "Bush Alienates Moderate Arabs," *Jerusalem Post*, April 26, 2004. "Prime Minister Ahmed Qureia told reporters at his home in the West Bank town of Abu Dis that the move 'kills the rights of the Palestinian people.'" Peter Slevin, "Bush Backs Israel on West Bank," *Washington Post*, April 15, 2004.

58. Lydia Saad, "Palestinians Have Little Faith in US as a Peace Broker," Gallup News Service, June 20, 2006, http://poll .gallup.com/content/default.aspx?ci=23377 [7/12/06].

59. Robert Zoellick, quoted in Anoushiravan Ehteshami,

"The Middle East: Between Ideology and Geo-politics," in *The Bush Doctrine and the War on Terrorism: Global Responses, Global Consequences*, ed. Mary Buckley and Robert Singh (London: Routledge, 2006), p. 107.

60. Two of the fundamental principles of *jus ad bellum* are the notions of last resort and proportionality, which assert that a state "may resort to war only if it has exhausted all plausible, peaceful alternatives to resolving the conflict in question, in particular diplomatic negotiation," and that prior to initiating a war, "a state must weigh the *universal* goods expected to result from it, such as securing the just cause, against the *universal* evils expected to result, notably casualties. Only if the benefits are proportional to, or 'worth,' the costs may the war action proceed. (The universal must be stressed, since often in war states only tally *their own* expected benefits and costs, radically discounting those accruing to the enemy and to any innocent third parties.)" Brian Orend, "War," in *The Stanford Encyclopedia of Philosophy*, ed. Edward N. Zalta (Winter 2005), http://plato.stanford.edu/archives/win2005/entries/war/ [7/26/06].

Chapter 5
Containment's Realism

1. The International Institute for Strategic Studies, *The Military Balance 2000–2001* (Oxford: Oxford University Press, 2000).

2. Alan Greenspan, Testimony before the Committee on the Budget, January 25, 2001, U.S. Senate, http://www.federalreserve.gov/Boarddocs/testimony/2001/20010125/default.htm [7/26/06].

3. See Greg Jaffe, "Rumsfeld's Vindication Promises a Change in Tactics, Deployment," *Wall Street Journal*, April 10, 2003; Thom Shanker and Eric Schmitt, "Rumsfeld Seeks Leaner Army, and a Full Term," *New York Times*, May 11, 2005; and Donald Rumsfeld, "Transforming the Military" *Foreign Affairs*, May/June 2002.

4. John Gaddis, *Strategies of Containment*, 2nd ed. (New York: Oxford University Press, 2005), p. 260.

5. "Katrina's Cost May Test GOP Harmony; Some Want Bush to Give Details on How U.S. Will Pay," *Washington Post*, September 21, 2005, p. A1.

6. See Mark Mazzetti, "Pentagon Says China Seeks to Extend Military Reach," *Los Angeles Times*, July 20, 2005, http://www.globalpolicy.org/empire/challenges/competitors/2005/0720pentagonchina.htm [6/13/06]; and "Military Power of the People's Republic of China 2006," Annual report of the Defense Department to Congress, http://www.defenselink.mil/pubs/pdfs/China%20Report%202006.pdf [6/13/06].

7. See Charles Ferguson, "Sparking a Buildup: U.S. Missile Defense and China's Nuclear Arsenal," *Arms Control Today*, March 2000, http://www.armscontrol.org/act/2000_03/cfmr00.asp [6/13/06]; and Sonia Joshi, "Pentagon Ready to Counter China Military Buildup with the Help of High Tech Armed India and Japan," *India Daily*, July 21, 2005, http://www.indiadaily.com/editorial/3707.asp [6/13/06].

8. Ron Suskind, *The One Percent Doctrine* (New York: Simon and Schuster, 2006).

9. "We will accept nothing less than total victory over the terrorists and their hateful ideology." George Bush, speech to the Veterans of Foreign Wars Convention, Salt Lake City, August 2005, http://www.whitehouse.gov/news/releases/2005/08/20050822-1.html [12/17/05]. This total victory claim was repeated in a series of speeches in subsequent months, but no account of what total victory could mean was ever supplied by the president.

10. See http://coursesa.matrix.msu.edu/~hst306/documents/indust.html [10/5/05].

11. See "Costs of War Quietly Surpass $300 Billion; Congress Approves Requests from the President and the Pentagon with Little Resistance and Adds a Few Unrelated Projects to

Boot," *Sacramento Bee*, April 25, 2005, p. A1. For evidence on hidden Iraq reconstruction costs, see James Glanz, "Audit Finds U.S. Hid Actual Cost of Iraq Projects," *New York Times*, July 30, 2006, pp. 1, 4.

12. In October of 2005 the Congressional Research Service reported that appropriations for the Iraq war had totaled approximately $251 billion, including $190 billion for the Department of Defense and $24.5 billion for Foreign Aid and Diplomatic Operations. See Amy Belasco, "The Cost of Iraq, Afghanistan and Enhanced Base Security since 9/11," Congressional Research Service, October 7, 2005, pp. 10 and 20, http://www.opencrs .com/rpts/RL33110_20051007.pdf [11/20/05].

13. War spending, known euphemistically as the "burn rate," includes the cost of fighting, as well as feeding and fueling the forces in the area, according to the military. See "Report: Terror War Costs $7B per Month," Associated Press, October 6, 2005, http://briefcaseman.gnn.tv/headlines/5343/Report_Terror_war_ costs_7B_per_month [11/20/05].

14. See Michael Renner, "Military Spending Near Record High," *World Watch* 5, no. 18 (September/October 2005). "The United States spends almost as much as the rest of the world combined: $455 billion in 2004, or 47% of the global total, reports SIPRI."

15. See Dara Cohen, Mariano-Florentino Cuellar, and Barry Weingast, "Crisis Bureaucracy: Homeland Security and the Political Design of Legal Mandates" (mimeo, Stanford University Department of Political Science, 2006).

16. Dan Eggen and Mary Beth Sheridan, "Anti-terror Funding Cut in DC and New York," *Washington Post*, June 1, 2006, p. A1, http://www.washingtonpost.com/wp-dyn/content/article/ 2006/05/31/AR2006053101364.html [7/31/06].

17. Robert Pape, "The Strategic Logic of Suicide Terrorism," *American Political Science Review* 97, no. 3 (August 2003): 343–61.

18. Matthew Brzezinski, "Red Alert," *Mother Jones* 29, no. 5

(September/October 2004). See also Richard A. Clarke, "Things Left Undone: Why Has an Administration That Talks So Much about Homeland Security Been So Unable to Secure the Homeland?" *Atlantic Monthly*, November, 2005, p. 38.

19. "Report of the Task Force for a Unified Security Budget for the United States, 2007," Center for Defense Information (May 2006), p. 13.

20. "In May, the active army shipped 5,039 recruits to boot camp, 25 percent less than its goal for the month." See "Military Struggling to Fill Ranks of Reserve Units," Associated Press, June 10, 2005.

21. See Mark Mazzetti, "The Conflict in Iraq: Army's Rising Promotion Rate Called Ominous; Experts Say the Quality of the Officer Corps Is Threatened as the Service Fights to Retain Leaders during Wartime and Fill New Command Slots," *Los Angeles Times*, January 30, 2006, http://www.truthout.org/cgi-bin/artman/exec/view.cgi/48/17349 [9/8/06].

22. See President Bush's Second Inaugural Address, January 2005, http://www.whitehouse.gov/news/releases/2005/01/20050120-1.html [5/25/06].

23. "The hope and intention is that over the coming years the bulk of the funds for Iraq's reconstruction will come from the Iraqis themselves—from oil revenues, recovered assets, international trade, and foreign direct investment. The funds the President has requested are designed to help Iraqis so they can generate the income, and security, necessary to rebuild their own country." Prepared testimony of Donald H. Rumsfeld before the House Appropriations Committee Defense Subcommittee, September 30, 2003, http://appropriations.senate.gov/hearmarkups/record.cfm?id=211939 [5/24/06].

24. In 1952 President Eisenhower campaigned against containment as "immoral" and "futile," advocating instead rollback of Soviet influence in Eastern Europe and setting the stage for America's military involvement in Southeast Asia. In fact, to

Kennan's chagrin, President Truman had already been moving in that direction for some time. See Kenneth Osgood, "Hearts and Minds: The Unconventional Cold War," *Journal of Cold War Studies* 4, no. 2 (Spring 2002): 89.

25. George W. Bush, January 2003 State of the Union, http://www.whitehouse.gov/news/releases/2003/01/20030128-19.html [4/15/06].

26. See Michael Dobbs, "U.S. Had Key Role in Iraq Buildup," *Washington Post*, December 30, 2002, p. A1.

27. Thomas Schelling, "Iranian Nuke Would Be a Suicide Bomb," *New Perspectives Quarterly* 23, no. 1 (Spring 2006), http://www.digitalnpq.org/archive/2006_winter/schelling.html [4/15/06].

28. See William Broad, "Sowing Death: How Japan Germ Terror Alerted the World," *New York Times*, May 26, 1998, p. A1.

29. See Federation of American Scientists Intelligence Resource Program, Militarily Critical Technologies List (MCTL), Part II: Weapons of Mass Destruction Technologies, Section 4—Chemical Weapons Technology, http://www.fas.org/irp/threat/mctl98-2/p2sec04.pdf [5/24/06].

30. See "Facts about Sarin," Centers for Disease Control, http://www.bt.cdc.gov/agent/sarin/basics/facts.asp [4/15/06].

31. "We don't want the smoking gun to be a mushroom cloud," said Condoleezza Rice in September of 2002. "Top Bush Officials Push Case against Saddam," September 8, 2002, http://archives.cnn.com/2002/ALLPOLITICS/09/08/iraq.debate/ [5/25/06].

32. "Iran, Its Neighbours and the Regional Crises," ed. Robert Lowe and Claire Spencer, The Royal Institute of International Affairs, Chatham House, London, 2006, p. 14.

33. George F. Will, "Transformation's Toll," *Washington Post*, July 18, 2006, p. A19; Michael Eisendadt, "Deter and Contain: Dealing with a Nuclear Iran," in *Getting Ready for a Nuclear-Ready Iran*, ed. Henry Sokolski and Patrick Clawson (Carlisle,

PA: Strategic Studies Institute, U.S. Army War College, 2005), pp. 225–55; Barry Posen, "We Can Live with a Nuclear Iran," *New York Times*, February 27, 2006, http://web.mit.edu/cis/posen.pdf [6/20/06]; Thomas L. Friedman, "Iraq II or Nuclear Iran?" *New York Times*, April 19, 2006, p. A21; and Richard Clark and Steven Simon, "Bombs That Would Backfire," *New York Times*, April 16, 2006, sec. 4, p. 13.

34. Richard Oppel Jr., "Iraq Official Says Iran Has Right to Atomic Power Goal," *New York Times*, May 27, 2006, p. A6.

35. Robert A. Pape, *Dying to Win: The Strategic Logic of Suicide Terrorism* (New York: Random House, 2005), pp. 248–49.

36. In a Fox News/Opinion Dynamics Poll conducted in October 2001, 50 percent of respondents believed that Saddam Hussein was "very likely" involved in the 9/11 attacks (conducted by Opinion Dynamics, October 31, 2001–November 1, 2001, and based on telephone interviews with a national registered voters sample of 900 [USODFOX.110201.R18]). A Gallup/CNN/*USA Today* poll in August 2002 found that 53 percent of respondents believed that Saddam Hussein was "personally involved in the September 11th terrorist attacks" (CNN, *USA Today*, Gallup, August 19, 2002–August 21, 2002, and based on telephone interviews with a national adult sample of 801 [USGALLUP.082302.R2]). See http://roperweb.ropercenter.uconn.edu/iPOLL/ [5/24/06].

37. Murray Waas and Brian Beutler, "What Bush Was Told about Iraq," *National Journal* 38, no. 9 (March 4, 2006): 40–43.

38. "Iran is prepared to launch attacks using long-range missiles, secret commando units, and terrorist allies planted around the globe in retaliation for any strike on the country's nuclear facilities, according to the new US intelligence assessments and military specialists." Bryan Bender, "Iran Is Prepared to Retaliate, Experts Warn," *Boston Globe*, February 16, 2006, http://www.boston.com/news/world/middleeast/articles/2006/02/12/iran_is_prepared_to_retaliate_experts_warn/ [5/24/06].

39. See Arthur Schlesinger, Jr., "Bush's Thousand Days," *Washington Post*, April 24, 2006, p. A17.

40. Marc Perelman, "New Front Sets Sights on Toppling Iran," *Forward News*, May 16, 2003, http://www.forward.com/issues/2003/03.05.16/news2.html [5/10/06].

41. Jenifer Johnson, "Regime Change in Iran Now in Bush's Sights," *Sunday Herald*, July 18, 2004, http://www.forward.com/issues/2003/03.05.16/news2.html [5/10/06].

42. See Michael Slackman and David E. Sanger, "US and Iranians Agree to Discuss Violence in Iraq," *New York Times*, March 17, 2006, p. A1, published the same week as the 2006 *National Security Strategy* was released.

43. See Seymour M. Hersh, "What Went Wrong: The C.I.A. and the Failure of American Intelligence," *New Yorker*, October 8, 2001, p. 34; Richard K. Betts, "Fixing Intelligence," *Foreign Affairs*, January/February 2002, pp. 43–59; and Douglas Jehl, "House Committee Says C.I.A. Is Courting Disaster by Mismanaging Its Human Spying," *New York Times*, June 25, 2004, p. A12.

44. Francis Fukuyama, *America at the Crossroads: Democracy, Power and the Neoconservative Legacy* (New Haven: Yale University Press, 2006), p. 176.

45. Robert O. Keohane, *After Hegemony: Cooperation and Discord in the World Political Economy* (Princeton: Princeton University Press, 1984), p. 247.

46. In 1994, John Bolton, whom President Bush would subsequently appoint as UN ambassador, said, "There is no such thing as the United Nations," and "If the U.N. Secretariat building in New York lost 10 stories, it wouldn't make a bit of difference." See Ian Williams, "Bush's Hatchet Man in the State Department," Salon.com, May 10, 2002, http://dir.salon.com/story/politics/feature/2002/05/10/bolton/index.html [5/25/06].

47. Keohane, *After Hegemony*, p. 259.

48. See Michael Byers, *War Law: Understanding International Law and Armed Conflict* (New York: Grove Press, 2005), pp. 147–

55, and Philippe Sands, *Lawless World: America and the Making and Breaking of Global Rules from FDR's Atlantic Charter to George W. Bush's Illegal War* (New York: Viking, 2005), pp. 174–256.

49. See United Nations Office of the Iraq Programme Oil-for-Food, Press Release, November 19, 2003, http://www.un.org/Depts/oip/cpmd/notices/terminationstatusoffunds031119.html [5/24/06].

50. "The Management of the United Nations Oil-for-Food Programme: Volume 1—The Report of the Committee," Independent Inquiry Committee into the United Nations Oil-for-Food Programme, Paul A. Volcker Chairman, September 7, 2005, www.iic-offp.org/documents/Sept05/Mgmt_V1.pdf [10/12/05].

51. See "Two Are Accused of Fraud in Iraqi Rebuilding Projects," *San Diego Union Tribune*, November 18, 2005, http://www.signonsandiego.com/uniontrib/20051118/news_1n18fraud.html [11/20/05].

52. See "Rep. Cunningham Pleads Guilty to Bribes, Resigns," *Los Angeles Times*, November 29, 2005, http://www.latimes.com/business/la-me-duke29nov29,0,7903329.story?coll=la-home-business [12/5/05].

53. U.S. military personnel reportedly viewed a Custer Battles spreadsheet accidentally left on the table during a meeting, indicating that the firm had charged the government $10 million for materials costing the firm $3.5 million. See CBS News, *60 Minutes*, February 12, 2006, http://www.cbsnews.com/stories/2006/02/09/60minutes/main1302378.shtml [3/4/06].

54. See Report by the Office of the Special Inspector General for Iraqi Reconstruction, Report Number 05–004, "Oversight of Funds Provided to Iraqi Ministries through the National Budget Process," January 30, 2005, http://www.sigir.mil/reports/pdf/audits/dfi_ministry_report.pdf [5/24/06].

55. Ali Allawi, Iraq's finance minister, has estimated that insurgents reap 40 to 50 percent of all oil-smuggling profits in Iraq. Robert F. Worth and James Glanz, "Oil Fuels Graft," *New*

York Times, February 5, 2006, p. 1. The extent to which this was hampering Iraqi reconstruction was becoming clear by mid-2006, when it surfaced that sabotage attacks that had crippled Iraq's oil pipelines were part of a lucrative moneymaking scheme by insurgents and criminal gangs to force the continued importation of oil that could then be stolen by truck drivers and sold on the black market. See James Glanz and Robert Worth, "Attacks on Iraq Oil Industry Aid Vast Smuggling Scheme," *New York Times*, June 4, 2006, p. A1.

56. David Rieff, "Were Sanctions Right?" *New York Times*, July 29, 2003, http://www.casi.org.uk/info/reiff.html [5/24/06].

57. John Lewis Gaddis, "After Containment: The Legacy of George Kennan in the Age of Terrorism," *New Republic*, April 25, 2005, p. 28.

58. U.S. ambassador to Baghdad April Glaspie met with Saddam Hussein shortly before the Iraqi invasion of Kuwait and reputedly told him, "We have no opinion on the Arab-Arab conflicts, like your border disagreement with Kuwait." See "Excerpts from Iraqi Document on Meeting with U.S. Envoy," *New York Times*, September 23, 1990.

59. U.S., British, and French forces began imposing a no-fly zone in southern Iraq beginning in April 1991, claiming authority under UN Security Council Resolution 688. A second no-fly zone was imposed in northern Iraq in 1992. The UN never recognized the no-fly zones. Stronger rules of engagement came into use in 1998.

60. Nicholas Kristof, "The Dear Leader's Boiling Cauldron," *New York Times*, July 11, 2006, p. A19.

61. President Bush's White House news conference, April 4, 2002, http://www.whitehouse.gov/news/releases/2002/04/20020404-1.html [5/6/06].

62. See Pape, *Dying to Win*; Mia Bloom, *Dying to Kill: The Allure of Suicide Terror* (New York: Columbia University Press, 2005); and Diego Gambetta, ed., *Making Sense of Suicide Missions* (Oxford: Oxford University Press, 2005).

63. Twenty-seven of them were communists or socialists with no commitment to religious extremism, three were Christians (one of whom was a female high school teacher with a college degree), and three were unidentifiable as to ideological or religious affiliation. All forty-one of them were born in Lebanon. Pape, *Dying to Win*, pp. 129–30; and Robert Pape, "Ground to a Halt," *New York Times*, August 3, 2006, p. A21.

64. See "Saudis Paid Bin Laden £200m," *Sunday Times* (UK), August 25, 2002.

65. Pape, *Dying to Win*, pp. 241–50, and Michael Scheuer, *Imperial Hubris: Why the West Is Losing the War on Terror* (Dulles, VA: Potomac Books, 2004), pp. 6–17.

66. See Charles M. Sennott and Charles A. Radin, "Arafat Illness Spurs Struggle for Influence: Key Palestinians Jockey over Possible Successors," *Boston Globe*, November 5, 2004, http://www.boston.com/news/world/articles/2004/11/05/arafat_illness_spurs_struggle_for_influence?pg=full [5/5/06].

67. A Palestinian Center for Policy and Survey Research poll in July of 2000 showed 68 percent of Palestinians believed Arafat's overall position at Camp David was "just right," while 15 percent believed he had compromised too much. PCPSR, "Public Opinion Poll #1," July 27–29, 2000, www.pcpsr.org/survey/polls/2000/pla.html [6/17/03]. Quoting Palestinian sources to the effect that "Arafat's ability to maneuver is nil," former secretary of state James Baker concluded, "[W]hat was not enough for Mr. Arafat was too much for many Israelis, to whom any agreement will be submitted by referendum." James A. Baker III, "Peace, One Step at a Time," *New York Times*, July 27, 2000, p. A25.

68. "I've asked why nobody saw it coming," said Ms Rice. See Steven R. Weisman, "Rice Admits U.S. Underestimated Hamas Strength," *New York Times*, January 30, 2006, p. A1.

69. For my own predictions in this regard, see Courtney Jung, Ellen Lust-Okar, and Ian Shapiro, "Problems and Prospects

for Democratic Settlements: South Africa as a Model for the Middle East and Northern Ireland?" *Politics and Society* 33, no. 2 (June 2005): 310–14.

70. In June of 2006 Vice President Cheney reasserted his "last throes" claim about the insurgency. See "Cheney Reasserts That Iraqi Insurgency Entered Its 'Last Throes' in May 2005," Think Progress, June 19, 2006, http://thinkprogress.org/2006/06/19/cheney-defends-last-throes-2 [6/20/06]. The number of Iraqi insurgents (as distinct from foreign fighters) is estimated to have grown from 3,000 in May of 2003 to 6,000 in May of 2004, to 16,000 in May of 2005, and 20,000 in May of 2006. Nina Kamp, Michael O'Hanlon, and Amy Unikewicz, "The State of Iraq: An Update," *New York Times*, June 16, 2006, http://www.nytimes.com/2006/06/16/opinion/16ohanlon.html?_r=1&n=Top%2fOpinion%2fEditorials%20and%20Op%2dEd%2fOp%2dEd%2fContributors&oref=slogin [6/20/06]. Nor was there any reduction in the rate at which U.S. soldiers were being killed—82 in April of 2006 and 79 in May. See "Iraq Coalition Casualties," http://icasualties.org/oif/ [6/21/06].

71. Yitzhak Rabin, "From Setbacks to Living Together," *New York Times*, September 5, 1993, p. 10.

72. Graham Usher, "The New Hamas: Between Resistance and Participation," *Middle East Report Online*, August 21, 2005, http://www.merip.org/mero/mero082105.html [6/6/06].

73. Ehud Yaari, "Fight Delay," *New Republic*, February 13, 2006, http://www.washingtoninstitute.org/templateC06.php?CID=899 [6/6/06].

74. See Ignacio Sánchez-Cuenca, "Nationalist Terrorism as a Constrained War of Attrition" (mimeo, Instituto Juan March and Universidad de Madrid, February 2005).

75. Poll #55, Jerusalem Media and Communication Center, December 2005, http://www.jmcc.org/publicpoll/results/2005/no55.pdf [7/12/06].

76. Chris McGreal, "Islamists Halt Attacks on Israel," *Guardian*,

January 24, 2005, http://www.guardian.co.uk/international/story/0,,1396958,00.html [6/20/06]; "Officials: Israel Ends Targeted Killings," NewsMax.com wires, January 26, 2005, http://www.newsmax.com/archives/articles/2005/1/26/11452.shtml [6/18/06].

77. Yaari, "Fight Delay."

78. See "Hamas Rejects Al-Qaeda's Support," March 5, 2005, http://news.bbc.co.uk/1/hi/world/middle_east/4776578.stm [5/17/06].

79. "Dealing with Hamas," ICG Middle East Report No. 21, Amman/Brussels, January 26, 2004, p. ii.

80. In the event, constitutionally mandated power sharing was accepted by the ANC for the interim (1994) constitution, but the National Party agreed to give it up in the final (1996) constitution in exchange for other concessions.

81. Interview with the author in Cape Town, December 8, 2004.

82. See Jung, Lust-Okar, and Shapiro, "Problems and Prospects," pp. 288–90, 297–301.

83. "Dealing with Hamas," p. 23.

84. See Shaul Mishal, "Hamas: The Agony of Victory," *Strategic Assessment* 9, no. 1 (April 2006): 6.

85. Steven Erlanger, "Hamas Fires Rockets into Israel, Ending 16-Month Truce," *New York Times*, June 11, 2006, p. A1.

86. Hazem al-Amin, "In the Palestinian Diaspora, They Joined Early . . . In the Territories, They Delayed in Receiving It" (pt. 1 of 2), *Al-Hayat*, April 7, 2006, http://english.daralhayat.com/Spec/04-2006/Article-20060407-74c40c9e-c0a8-10ed-0105-0034e1a86f7c/story.html [6/14/06]; and "In the Palestinian Diaspora . . . 'International Jihad' Accelerates Its Steps in the West Bank and Gaza, after 'National Jihad' Formed Its Government" (pt. 2 of 2), *Al-Hayat*, April 10, 2006, http://english.daralhayat.com/Spec/04-2006/Article-20060410-84272b88-c0a8-10ed-0105-0034bc562c62/story.html

[6/14/06]. See also Khaled Abu Toameh and Larry Derfner, "A Tough Neighborhood: Is Al Qaeda Branching Out to the Palestinian Territories?" *U.S. News and World Report*, May 15, 2006, http://www.usnews.com/usnews/news/articles/060515/15mideast.htm [6/14/06].

87. See Jung, Lust-Okar, and Shapiro, "Problems and Prospects," pp. 297–301.

88. Olivier Roy, *Globalized Islam: The Search for a New Ummah* (New York: Columbia University Press, 2004), pp. 293–94.

89. Susan Glasser and Walter Pincus, "Seized Letter Outlines Al Qaeda Goals in Iraq," *Washington Post*, October 12, 2005, p. A13. Zarqawi denied the letter's authenticity.

90. Roy, *Globalized Islam*, pp. 293–95.

91. See "Terrorist Financing: Report of an Independent Task Force Sponsored by the Council on Foreign Relations," Council on Foreign Relations Report, Maurice R. Greenberg (Chair), William F. Wechsler and Lee S. Wolosky (Project Co-Directors), October 2002, http://www.cfr.org/publication.html?id=5080 [5/24/06].

92. William F. Wechsler, "Follow the Money," *Foreign Affairs*, July/August, 2001, pp. 40–57.

93. See Jennifer Quinn and Paul Haven, "Money Trail Probed in Foiled Plot," *Airport Business*, August 12, 2006, http://www.airportbusiness.com/article/article.jsp?siteSection=1&id=7575 [9/8/06].

94. See "Update on the Global Campaign against Terrorist Financing," Council on Foreign Relations, June 15, 2004, http://www.cfr.org/content/publications/attachments/Revised_Terrorist_Financing.pdf [6/12/06].

95. Gaddis, "After Containment," p. 28.

96. Senator John McCain speaking on the *Imus in the Morning* radio program, WFAN, New York, July 26, 2006, http://www.msnbc.msn.com/id/9877519/ [7/26/06].

97. The first PLO bases were established in Egypt, Iraq, and

Syria in 1964. PLO "secure bases" were developed in the late 1960s in the East Bank of Jordan, then in southern Lebanon, with a political base in Syria. The PLO was expelled from Jordan in 1970–71. Following the evacuation of the PLO from Beirut in June 1982, PLO fighters were distributed in Algeria, Tunisia, the Sudan, Yemen, and Iraq. See Yezid Sayigh, "Palestinian Armed Struggle: Means and Ends," *Journal of Palestine Studies* 16, no. 1 (1986): 95–112, and Fuad Jabber, "The Arab Regimes and the Palestinian Revolution, 1967–71," *Journal of Palestine Studies* 2, no. 2 (1973): 79–101, and http://www.globalsecurity.org/military/world/para/plo_military.htm [11/18/05].

98. Pauline Jones-Luong and Ellen Lust-Okar, "Rethinking the Relationship between Transnational and National Islamists" (paper presented at the conference on Democracy, Governance, and Identity, University of Michigan, May 5–6, 2006).

99. See Zecharia Kahn, "The Hamas Gamble," *Journal of Middle Eastern Geopolitics* 2, no. 1 (January/March 2006): 85–94.

100. "Update on the Global Campaign against Terrorist Financing."

101. Written testimony of David D. Aufhauser, General Counsel before the Committee on Banking, Housing, and Urban Affairs, United States Senate, September 25, 2003, http://www.ustreas.gov/press/releases/js760.htm [6/12/06].

102. Michael Slackman and David E. Sanger, "US and Iranians Agree to Discuss Violence in Iraq," *New York Times*, March 17, 2006, p. A1.

103. Peter Katzenstein and Robert Keohane, eds., *Anti-Americanism in World Politics* (Ithaca: Cornell University Press, forthcoming), manuscript pp. 12–13.

104. Nina Kamp, Michael O'Hanlon, and Amy Unikewicz, "The State of Iraq: An Update," *New York Times*, June 16, 2006, http://www.nytimes.com/2006/06/16/opinion/16ohanlon.html?_r=1&n=Top%2fOpinion%2fEditorials%20and%20Op%2dEd%2fOp%2dEd%2fContributors&oref=slogin [6/20/06].

105. David Cortright and George Lopez, "Bombs, Carrots, and Sticks: The Use of Incentives and Sanctions," *Arms Control Today*, March 2005, http://www.armscontrol.org/act/2005_03/Cortright.asp#bio [6/18/06].

106. George Lopez and David Cortright, "Containing Iraq: Sanctions Worked," *Foreign Affairs*, July/August 2004, http://www.foreignaffairs.org/20040701faessay83409/george-a-lopez-david-cortright/containing-iraq-sanctions-worked.html [6/10/06].

107. "Patterns of Global Terrorism," U.S. State Department, April 1996, http://www.fas.org/irp/threat/terror_96/overview.html [6/10/06].

108. "Lockerbie Crash Timeline," CNN.com, September 12, 2003, http://www.cnn.com/2003/WORLD/europe/08/14/lockerbie.timeline/ [6/10/06].

109. "Libya Pays France Plane Bomb Damages," BBC News, July 16, 1999, http://news.bbc.co.uk/1/hi/world/europe/396254.stm [6/18/06].

110. "Background Note: Libya," U.S. Department of State: Bureau of Near Eastern Affairs, November 2005, http://www.state.gov/r/pa/ei/bgn/5425.htm [6/18/06].

111. Flynt Leverett, "Why Libya Gave Up on the Bomb," *New York Times*, January 23, 2004, http://www.mtholyoke.edu/acad/intrel/bush/libya.htm [6/10/06].

112. Andrew Solomon, "Circle of Fire: Libya's Reformers Dream of Rejoining the World," *New Yorker*, May 8, 2006, http://www.newyorker.com/fact/content/articles/060508fa_fact3 [6/10/06].

113. "Patterns of Global Terrorism: Libya 2002 Overview," MITP Terrorism Knowledge Base, http://www.tkb.org/MorePatterns.jsp?countryCd=LY&year=2002 [6/10/06].

114. Jonathan Freedland, "The War's Silver Lining," *Guardian*, March 2, 2005, http://www.guardian.co.uk/comment/story/0,3604,1428372,00.html [7/29/06].

115. "We didn't need to go to war with Iraq to liberate

Lebanon because it was the Lebanese who liberated Lebanon. . . . It was people power. . . . They came into the streets not because of the U.S. in Iraq but because of what the Syrians had done for the past 30 years." Martin Indyk, interview with the author, July 28, 2006.

116. Charles Glass, "Is Syria Next?" *London Review of Books* 25, no. 4 (July 24, 2003), http://www.lrb.co.uk/v25/n14/glas01_.html [7/29/06].

117. The exception was a brief attempt at a comprehensive settlement in 1983. U.S. Secretary of State George Shultz negotiated the "May 17 Agreement" among Lebanon, Israel, and the major Arab regimes—except Syria. Under it, all foreign forces, Syrian, Israeli, and multinational, would have left Lebanon. But it was never implemented.

118. Fida Narsallah, "Syria after Ta'if: Lebanon and the Lebanese in Syrian Politics," in *Contemporary Syria: Liberalization between Cold War and Cold Peace*, ed. Eberhard Kienle (New York: British Academic Press, 1994), pp. 135–36.

119. Martin Indyk, interview with the author, July 28, 2006.

120. Resolution 1559 (September 2, 2004), http://daccess-dds.un.org/doc/UNDOC/GEN/N04/498/92/PDF/N0449892.pdf?OpenElement [7/29/06].

121. In March of 2005 an Israeli ex-general predicted to me off the record that this would occur. Israel had acquiesced in the Syrian presence in Lebanon just because the Israelis recognized this reality.

122. Paul Salem, interview with the author, July 28, 2006.

123. Martin Indyk, interview with the author, July 28, 2006, and follow-up correspondence, July 30, 2006.

124. In the short run at least Hezbollah leader Hassan Nasrallah's stock rose in Lebanon and across the region, even in Sunni regimes, following the Israeli invasion in July of 2006. Nasrallah was able to claim credit for standing up to an Israeli

military that was inflicting large numbers of casualties on Lebanese civilians. See Neil MacFarquhar, "Tide of Arab Opinion Turns to Support for Hezbollah," *New York Times*, July 28, 2006, pp. A1, A16.

125. An April 2006 NBC/WSJ poll showed 57 percent of Americans disapproving of the "job that George W. Bush is doing as president." http://msnbcmedia.msn.com/i/msnbc/sections/news/060424_NBC-WSJ_Poll.pdf [6/16/06]. A *USA Today/Gallup* poll conducted June 9–11, 2006, revealed 60 percent of Americans disapproving of the situation in Iraq. Joseph Carroll, "Gallup Analysis: Bush Job Approval on Key Issues," Gallup Poll, June 14, 2006, http://poll.gallup.com/content/default.aspx?ci=23317 [6/20/06].

Chapter 6
Democracy for Containment

1. Bob Woodward, *Plan of Attack* (New York: Simon & Schuster, 2004), p. 35.

2. President Bush's address to U.S. troops at Osan Air Base in Osan, Korea, November 19, 2005, http://www.whitehouse.gov/news/releases/2005/11/20051119-5.html [9/6/06].

3. See chap. 5, n. 103.

4. The Marshall Plan cost American taxpayers some $13 billion over four years starting in 1947. See http://www.usaid.gov/multimedia/video/marshall/study.html. [11/20/05]. Assuming an inflation rate of 800 percent (see http://inflationdata.com/inflation/Inflation_Rate/InflationCalculator.asp [11.20/05]), that is about $104 billion in 2005 dollars. By 2005 the prospects for the Iraqi economy were so poor that the Paris Club had written off 80 percent of its debt. Global News Wire–Asia Africa Intelligence Wire, BBC Monitoring/BBC Source: Financial Times Information Limited, http://web.lexis-nexis.com/universe/document?_

m=5f58c1c3156a3a632d5ae0b58af3aea8&_docnum=17&wchp=
dGLbVtz-zSkVb&_md5=15da148b686d7d7d1a114c37b9708078
[9/8/06].

5. Andrew Grice, "Blair Flies to Bush's Side to Mount Strong
Defense of Iraq Invasion," *Independent*, May 22, 2006, p. 4.

6. See, among others, Immanuel Kant, *Perpetual Peace* (Indi-
anapolis: Bobbs-Merrill, 1957); Bruce Russett, *Grasping the
Democratic Peace: Principles for a Post–Cold War World* (Princeton:
Princeton University Press, 1993); and Michael W. Doyle, "Kant,
Liberal Legacies and Foreign Affairs," *Philosophy and Public Affairs*
12, no. 3 (1983).

7. Edward Mansfield and Jack Snyder, *Electing to Fight: Why
Emerging Democracies Go to War* (Cambridge, MA: MIT Press,
2005).

8. Such assertions hinge on pooled cross-national comparisons. According to some, such comparisons are inherently
flawed owing to the extent of cross-sectional variability. For an
overview of the debate over the statistical analysis of militarized
disputes between countries, see Donald P. Green, Soo Yeon Kim,
and David H. Yoon, "Dirty Pool," *International Organization* 55,
no. 2 (Spring 2001): 441–68; Nathanial Beck and Jonathan N.
Katz, "What to Do (and Not to Do) with Time-Series-Cross-
Section Data," *American Political Science Review* 89, no. 3 (1995):
634–47. As Michael Doyle notes, these data difficulties confront
almost all generalizations in international relations, and there is
considerable case-study support for the democratic peace hy-
pothesis. Michael Doyle, *Ways of War and Peace* (New York: W. W.
Norton, 1997), pp. 251–300.

9. Stathis Kalyvas and Ignacio Sánchez-Cuenca, "Killing
without Dying: The Absence of Suicide Missions," in *Making Sense
of Suicide Missions*, ed. Diego Gambetta (Oxford: Oxford University Press, 2005), p. 228.

10. Guardian Unlimited, interview with Madeleine Albright,

October 30, 2003, http://www.guardian.co.uk/usa/story/0, 12271,1073881,00.html [5/27/06].

11. "Punishing Saddam," *60 Minutes*, May 12, 1996. See also Madeleine Albright, *Madame Secretary: A Memoir* (New York: Miramax Books, 2005), p. 275.

12. Steven Roberts, "Senate, 78–21, Overrides Reagan's Veto and Imposes Sanctions on South Africa," *New York Times*, October 3, 1986, p. A1. On the ANC's support for sanctions, see http://www.anc.org.za/ancdocs/pr/1980s/pr881010a.html [6/16/06].

13. Nikolay Marinov, "Do Economic Sanctions Destabilize Country Leaders?" *American Journal of Political Science* 49, no. 3 (July 2005): 564–76.

14. Steven Lee Meyers, "Trade vs. Rights: A US Debate with Burmese Focus," *New York Times*, March 5, 1997, p. A8; John Feffer, "Time to Lift North Korea's Quarantine," Yale Global Online, June 8, 2006, http://yaleglobal.yale.edu/display .article?id=7535 [9/8/06].

15. See Laura Rozen, "The Revolution Next Time," *Boston Globe*, October 10, 2004, http://www.boston.com/news/globe/ ideas/articles/2004/10/10/the_revolution_next_time?mode=PF [6/18/06].

16. Peter Katzenstein and Robert Keohane, eds., *Anti-Americanism in World Politics* (Ithaca: Cornell University Press, forthcoming), manuscript pp. 12–13.

17. See http://www.americanprogress.org/atf/cf/{E9245 FE4-9A2B-43C7-A521-5D6FF2E06E03}/INTEGRATED_ POWER.PDF [11/21/05].

18. See the review of *The Withering Away of the Totalitarian State . . . and Other Surprises*, by Jeane J. Kirkpatrick (Lanham, MD: AEI Press, 1990), by Saul Landau in *Political Science Quarterly* 106, no. 3 (Autumn 1991): 546–48.

19. See chap. 4, n. 41, above.

20. Ewen MacAskill, Simon Tisdall, and Robert Tait, "Lone Jewish MP Confronts Ahmadinejad on Holocaust but Stresses Loyalty to Iran," *Guardian*, June 28, 2006, http://www.guardian .co.uk/iran/story/0,,1807497,00.html [7/26/06].

21. See Adam Przeworski et al., *Democracy and Development: Political Institutions and Well-Being in the World, 1950–1990* (Cambridge: Cambridge University Press, 2000), chap. 2, and Ian Shapiro, *The State of Democratic Theory* (Princeton: Princeton University Press, 2003), pp. 78–103.

22. They can, however, be conquered, as democratic France was in 1940.

23. Przeworski et al., *Democracy and Development*, pp. 106–17.

Chapter 7
Our Present Peril

1. See Michael Gordon and Bernard Trainor, *Cobra II: The Inside Story of the Invasion and Occupation of Iraq* (New York: Pantheon Books, 2006).

2. Charles Babington, "Hawkish Democrat Calls for Pullout," *Washington Post*, November 18, 2005, http://www .washingtonpost.com/wp-dyn/content/article/2005/11/17/ AR2005111700794.html [12/14/05].

3. A November 2005 a CNN/*USA Today*/Gallup poll showed an alarming 63 percent of the American public disapproving of President Bush's Iraq policy. The following month the same poll found that 58 percent believed that Bush had no clear plan for victory in Iraq, with only 38 percent believing that he did. http://www.cnn.com/2005/POLITICS/12/12/bush .iraq.poll/index.html [12/13/05].

4. "War Quotes: Literary Quotes about War and Virtually Everything Else," http://quotes.prolix.nu/War/ [6/15/06].

5. "Ambition must be made to counteract ambition. . . . If

men were angels, no government would be necessary. If angels were to govern men, neither external nor internal controls on government would be necessary. In framing a government which is to be administered by men over men, the great difficulty lies in this: you must first enable the government to control the governed; and in the next place oblige it to control itself. A dependence on the people is, no doubt, the primary control on the government; but experience has taught mankind the necessity of auxiliary precautions." Alexander Hamilton, James Madison, and John Jay, *The Federalist Papers* (New York: Mentor, 1961), pp. 324–25.

6. On the biological weapons labs fiasco, see Dana Milbank and Walter Pincus, "Asterisks Dot White House Argument," *Washington Post*, November 12, 2005, p. A1. On the administration's refusal to listen to intelligence reports questioning the Iraqi WMD programs, see former CIA official Tyler Drumheller's interview with Ed Bradley, "A Spy Speaks Out," *60 Minutes*, April 3, 2006, http://www.cbsnews.com/stories/2006/04/21/60minutes/main 1527749.shtml [5/6/06].

7. Murray Waas and Brian Beutler, "What Bush Was Told about Iraq," *National Journal* 38, no. 9 (March 4, 2006): 40–43.

8. Joby Warrick, "Lacking Biolabs, Trailers Carried Case for War; Administration Pushed Notion of Banned Iraqi Weapons despite Evidence to Contrary," *Washington Post*, April 12, 2006, p. A1.

9. See http://www.rawstory.com/news/2006/Senator_ Kerry_Attacks_on_dissent_cheap_0422.html [4/23/2006].

10. Jonathan Landay, "Iraq Assessments Given to Public Stripped of Dissent, Doubt; Once Classified Records Show Wariness in Intelligence Community," *Milwaukee Journal Sentinel*, February 15, 2004, p. A12.

11. Milbank and Pincus, "Asterisks Dot White House Argument," p. A1.

12. The Boland Amendment prohibited covert assistance for

military operations in Nicaragua. See http://thomas.loc.gov/cgi-bin/bdquery/z?d098:HR02968:@@@L&summ2=m&|TOM:/bss/d098query.html [6/16/06].

13. See John Gaddis, *Strategies of Containment* (New York: Oxford University Press, 1982), pp. 272–306.

14. See Arthur Schlesinger, Jr., "Bush's Thousand Days," *Washington Post*, April 24, 2006, p. A17.

15. Twenty-nine Democratic senators voted to authorize war in Iraq, as did eighty-one Democratic representatives. See "Senate Approves Iraq War Resolution," CNN.com, October 11, 2002, http://archives.cnn.com/2002/ALLPOLITICS/10/11/iraq.us/ [11/13/05], and "How the House Voted on Iraq Resolution," Newsmax.com, October 11, 2002, http://www.newsmax.com/archives/articles/2002/10/10/203425.shtml [11/13/05].

16. Carla Marinucci, "Kerry Slams Bush on Terror, Democrat Says He'd Send 40,000 More Troops Overseas," *San Francisco Chronicle*, February 28, 2004, http://www.sfgate.com/cgi-bin/article.cgi?f=/c/a/2004/02/28/DemocratS.TMP [6/20/06].

17. By 1968 President Johnson had ended up with almost half a million American troops in Vietnam trying unsuccessfully to "finish the job" that President Kennedy had begun with 3,500 troops in 1965. Gaddis, *Strategies of Containment*, p. 246.

18. For an account of the Democratic Leadership Council and its adoption of "triangulation," see Michael Graetz and Ian Shapiro, *Death by a Thousand Cuts: The Fight over Taxing Inherited Wealth* (Princeton: Princeton University Press, 2005), pp. 262–64.

19. The Personal Responsibility and Work Opportunity Reconciliation Act of 1996, http://thomas.loc.gov/cgi-bin/query/z?c104:H.R.3734.ENR:htm [11/13/05].

20. In 1974, Democrats controlled 37 state legislatures, the highest number for either party since 1938. The party's control of state legislatures declined steadily until 2004 when they controlled 17. See "Table of Partisan Control of State Legislatures, 1938–2004," National Conference of State Legislatures, http://www.ncsl.org/programs/legman/elect/hstptyct.htm

[11/20/05]. Similarly, Democratic governorships have mostly decreased over the same period from a high of 37 in 1978 to 22 in 2004—up from the 18 they had held in 1996 and 2000. See "35-Year Gubernatorial Trends," Council of State Governments, http://www.csg.org/CSG/States/elections/2004/gubernatorial+trends.htm [11/20/05].

21. Triangulation might seem to have been more successful for New Labour, though this can easily be exaggerated. Blair's large parliamentary majorities are partly explained by the Tories' complete collapse in Scotland, their tearing civil war over Europe, redistricting changes that have been very harsh for them, and, as with Clinton, a leader whose Teflon charisma might well turn out not to be bequeathable.

22. John Kerry opposed the privatization of Social Security and tax breaks for wealthy Americans during the 2004 campaign, but he consistently played up his supposed credentials as a fiscal conservative. He also repeatedly said he favored tort reform—despite the fact that he had voted several times in the Senate not to restrict medical tort liability. See John Kerry on VoteMatch.com, http://www.issues2000.org/John_Kerry_VoteMatch.htm [11/13/05]; "John Kerry vs. John Kerry on Legal Reform," Center for Individual Freedom, October 14, 2004, http://www.cfif.org/htdocs/freedomline/current/in_our_opinion/kerry_vs_john_kerry.htm [11/13/05].

23. The story of how this happened is told in Graetz and Shapiro, *Death by a Thousand Cuts*.

24. See ibid., pp. 99–106, 221–38, 253–65.

25. For a lucid account of this history, see Andrew Bacevich, *The New American Militarism: How Americans Are Seduced by War* (New York: Oxford University Press, 2005), pp. 69–174.

26. The exception might be said to be the Bush administration's failed Social Security reform at the start of the second term. But the credit for this goes more to the AARP than to Democrats on Capitol Hill.

27. See Jane Mayer, "Outsourcing Torture," *New Yorker*, Feb-

ruary 14, 2005, and Karen DeYoung, "U.S. Toughens Warnings to Syria on Iraq, Other Issues," *Washington Post*, April 15, 2003.

28. H.J. Res 114, 107th Cong., 2nd sess., October 11, 2002, http://thomas.loc.gov/cgi-bin/bdquery/z?d107:HJ00114: @@@L&summ2=m& [11/13/05].

29. For an overview of Hillary Clinton's national security position, including several recent speeches, see http://clinton .senate.gov/issues/nationalsecurity/ [11/13/05]. See also Charles Hurt, "Hillary Goes Conservative on Immigration," *Washington Times*, December 13, 2004, http://washingtontimes.com/national/ 20041213-124920-6151r.htm [11/13/05]. John Nichols, a commentator in the *Nation*, has remarked, "There is nothing progressive, nor even liberal about Hillary Clinton's stance on national security issues—she wants to 'stay the course' in Iraq, she's backed even the most over-the-top spending allocations for the war, she's been a supporter of the Patriot Act and other assaults on civil liberties and she's frequently more in line with the Bush Administration's approach on national security issues than a number of Senate Republicans," August 9, 2005, http://www .thenation.com/blogs/thebeat?bid=1&pid=11167 [11/13/05].

Index